| Health Care

'S AND FREEDOMS

I Health Care

Noël Merino
Book Editor

GREENHAVEN PRESS
A part of Gale, Cengage Learning

GALE
CENGAGE Learning·

Farmington Hills, Mich • San Francisco • New York • Waterville, Maine
Meriden, Conn • Mason, Ohio • Chicago

Elizabeth Des Chenes, *Director, Content Strategy*
Douglas Dentino, *Manager, New Product*

© 2015 Greenhaven Press, a part of Gale, Cengage Learning

WCN: 01-100-101

LIBRARY OF CONGRESS CATALOGING-IN-PUBLICATION DATA

Health care / Noël Merino, book editor.
        pages cm. -- (Teen rights and freedoms)
    Includes bibliographical references and index.
    ISBN 978-0-7377-7000-1 (hardback)
    1. Medical care--Law and legislation--United States--Juvenile literature. I. Merino, Noël, editor of compilation.
    KF3821.H432 2014
    344.7304'1--dc23
                                                                        2014010792

Printed in the United States of America
1 2 3 4 5 6 7 18 17 16 15 14

Contents

Foreword   1

Introduction   4

Chronology   7

1. **Minors' Rights Regarding Health Care Have Expanded in Past Decades**   11

   Gale Encyclopedia of Everyday Law

   The author gives an overview of how the rights of minors to make their own medical decisions have evolved in the past sixty years.

2. **The Right to Privacy Protects a Minor's Right to Access Contraceptives**   19
   The Supreme Court's Decision

   William J. Brennan Jr.

   The US Supreme Court rules that prohibiting the sale of birth control, or contraceptives, to minors violates their constitutional rights.

3. **Parental Consent for a Minor's Abortion Cannot Be Absolute**   26
   The Supreme Court's Decision

   Lewis F. Powell Jr.

   The US Supreme Court rules that parental consent for a minor's abortion can be required as long as there is an alternative judicial procedure for granting permission.

4. **Parental Involvement Laws for Abortion Protect Minors and Parents**   35

Mary E. Harned

An attorney argues that laws requiring parental consent or parental notification for a minor's abortion protect the well-being of minors and the rights of parents.

5. **A Hotline Director Explains Why She Helps Minors Obtain Abortions**   45

Personal Narrative

Tina Hester

The executive director of a nonprofit organization contends that she helps young women in Texas navigate the increasingly complex path to getting a legal abortion.

6. **Commitment of Minors for Psychiatric Care Does Not Violate Due Process**   48

The Supreme Court's Decision

Warren E. Burger

The US Supreme Court decides that a parent or guardian can commit a minor to a mental institution if medically certified, even if the minor opposes their decision.

7. **Mature Minors Have the Right to Consent to or Refuse Medical Care**   59

The Illinois Supreme Court's Decision

Howard C. Ryan

The Supreme Court of Illinois finds that there is a constitutional and common-law basis for allowing certain mature minors to refuse medical treatment.

8. **Religious Freedom Does Not Permit Parents to Deny Children Life-Saving Treatment**   69
   The Wisconsin Supreme Court's Decision

   Shirley S. Abrahamson

   The Wisconsin Supreme Court determines that a criminal statute outlawing homicide is not null because of a statute allowing certain faith-based healing.

9. **Religious Freedom Protects Parents' Health Care Decisions for Children**   82
   A.M. Rogers

   An attorney argues that to prosecute parents for their decisions about health care for their children without prosecuting doctors for their decisions involves a double standard.

10. **Religious Freedom Does Not Allow a Parent to Refuse Medical Treatment for a Child**   94
    R. Albert Mohler Jr.

    A theologian argues that the religious rights of parents do not permit them to refuse urgently needed medical care for their children.

11. **A Parent Recounts Her Decision to Refuse Medical Treatment for Religious Reasons**   100
    Personal Narrative

    Rita Swan

    An organization president who previously was a member of a faith-healing religion contends that children's health care should be a legal duty.

12. **Medicine, Minors, and Parents: Diminishing Parental Rights in Medicine**   109
    Mary Summa

An attorney contends that parental rights are under attack, threatening the well-being of children, the strength of the family, and the stability of society.

Organizations to Contact 122
For Further Reading 127
Index 131

Foreword

> *"In the truest sense freedom cannot be bestowed, it must be achieved."*
> *Franklin D. Roosevelt,*
> *September 16, 1936*

The notion of children and teens having rights is a relatively recent development. Early in American history, the head of the household—nearly always the father—exercised complete control over the children in the family. Children were legally considered to be the property of their parents. Over time, this view changed, as society began to acknowledge that children have rights independent of their parents, and that the law should protect young people from exploitation. By the early twentieth century, more and more social reformers focused on the welfare of children, and over the ensuing decades advocates worked to protect them from harm in the workplace, to secure public education for all, and to guarantee fair treatment for youths in the criminal justice system. Throughout the twentieth century, rights for children and teens—and restrictions on those rights—were established by Congress and reinforced by the courts. Today's courts are still defining and clarifying the rights and freedoms of young people, sometimes expanding those rights and sometimes limiting them. Some teen rights are outside the scope of public law and remain in the realm of the family, while still others are determined by school policies.

Each volume in the Teen Rights and Freedoms series focuses on a different right or freedom and offers an anthology of key essays and articles on that right or freedom and the responsibilities that come with it. Material within each volume is drawn from a diverse selection of primary and secondary sources— journals, magazines, newspapers, nonfiction books, organization newsletters, position papers, speeches, and government documents, with a particular emphasis on Supreme Court and lower court decisions. Volumes also include first-person narratives from young people and others involved in teen rights issues, such as parents and educators. The material is selected and arranged to highlight all the major social and legal controversies relating to the right or freedom under discussion. Each selection is preceded by an introduction that provides context and background. In many cases, the essays point to the difference between adult and teen rights, and why this difference exists.

Many of the volumes cover rights guaranteed under the Bill of Rights and how these rights are interpreted and protected in regard to children and teens, including freedom of speech, freedom of the press, due process, and religious rights. The scope of the series also encompasses rights or freedoms, whether real or perceived, relating to the school environment, such as electronic devices, dress, Internet policies, and privacy. Some volumes focus on the home environment, including topics such as parental control and sexuality.

Numerous features are included in each volume of Teen Rights and Freedoms:

- An annotated **table of contents** provides a brief summary of each essay in the volume and highlights court decisions and personal narratives.

- An **introduction** specific to the volume topic gives context for the right or freedom and its impact on daily life.

- A brief **chronology** offers important dates associated with the right or freedom, including landmark court cases.

- **Primary sources**—including personal narratives and court decisions—are among the varied selections in the anthology.

- **Illustrations**—including photographs, charts, graphs, tables, statistics, and maps—are closely tied to the text and chosen to help readers understand key points or concepts.

- An annotated list of **organizations to contact** presents sources of additional information on the topic.
- A **for further reading** section offers a bibliography of books, periodical articles, and Internet sources for further research.
- A comprehensive subject **index** provides access to key people, places, events, and subjects cited in the text.

Each volume of Teen Rights and Freedoms delves deeply into the issues most relevant to the lives of teens: their own rights, freedoms, and responsibilities. With the help of this series, students and other readers can explore from many angles the evolution and current expression of rights both historic and contemporary.

Introduction

The US government and state governments traditionally have recognized the right of parents to make decisions about health care for their children, with the reasoning that prior to reaching the age of majority (which is eighteen years in most states), children lack the experience and judgment to make fully informed decisions. There are exceptions to this rule, such as in the case of medical emergencies or when a minor is emancipated by marriage or other circumstances. Courts in some states have adopted what is called the mature minor rule, which allows a minor who is mature enough to understand proposed medical treatment to consent to such treatment without parental involvement. Additionally, over the last few decades, many states have passed laws explicitly authorizing minors to consent to health care related to abortion, drug and alcohol abuse, and mental health care without necessarily notifying parents or getting their consent.

The expansion in recent decades of minors' decision-making regarding health care without parental involvement is partially the result of US Supreme Court rulings. The court extended the constitutional right to privacy to a minor's decision to get an abortion or to obtain contraceptives in *Planned Parenthood of Central Missouri v. Danforth* (1976) and *Carey v. Population Services International* (1977), respectively. Almost four decades later, the issue remains contentious, particularly regarding the appropriate level of parental involvement. Although in 1979, in *Bellotti v. Baird*, the court ruled that parental consent for a minor's abortion can be required as long as there is a legal alternative for mature minors, there are still competing opinions about whether current state laws go too far or not far enough in allowing minors to make health care decisions without the involvement of their parents.

Another controversy regarding the health care decisions of minors involves parental refusal of medical treatment for children based on religious belief. Members of certain religious groups—such as Jehovah's Witnesses, Christian Scientists, and certain fundamentalist Christians—refuse some medical treatment for themselves and their children based on their belief that such medical intervention is forbidden by God. When the refusal of medical treatment results in the injury or death of a child, parents have sometimes been charged with criminal abuse, neglect, or manslaughter. The state courts' reactions to such cases have varied. In 1988, in *Walker v. Superior Court*, the Supreme Court of California upheld the conviction of a Christian Scientist mother found guilty of involuntary manslaughter after her daughter died of untreated meningitis. But in 1992, in *Hermanson v. State*, the Supreme Court of Florida determined that parents were not criminally liable for the death of a child caused by the failure to seek medical treatment for their diabetic daughter, finding a religious exemption law to apply to their case.

The Hermansons did not seek medical treatment for their daughter because, as members of the First Church of Christ, Scientist, they believed in healing by spiritual means and were guided by their church leaders to use prayer—or faith healing—for their daughter's illness. They relied on prayer in the treatment of Amy Hermanson's ever-worsening condition until the day she died. Medical experts agree that Amy's life could have been easily saved by simple medical intervention. The state supreme court allowed the Hermansons an exemption to their criminal prosecution based on the presence of a Florida child abuse statute containing a spiritual treatment accommodation provision that stated a parent forgoing medical care of a child for religious reasons "may not be considered abusive or neglectful for that reason alone." The State argued that the statute did not absolve parents of criminal charges, but the court determined that this spiritual treatment accommodation could have been understood by the Hermansons to absolve them of criminal liability. The court refused to endorse the view that spiritual treatment was not considered child abuse or neglect until the point at which it caused harm or death to the child, charging the legislature with the task of making the statutes clearer in this regard.

The Wisconsin Supreme Court recently decided a case similar to *Hermanson v. State* in precisely the opposite manner, finding the parents criminally culpable for the death of their diabetic daughter who did not receive any medical treatment, as discussed in this volume. This issue will likely continue to see varied outcomes in different states in the absence of a federal law or US Supreme Court decision on the matter. The right to health care of children is at issue here when the child is too young to consent or when the child's wishes conflict with that of the adult. But an interesting issue is also raised when a minor desires to refuse health care based on his or her religion, as is discussed in this volume.

In the United States, the rights and freedoms of minors to make health care decisions have evolved in recent decades. By presenting the US Supreme Court's decisions, state court decisions, social commentary, and personal narratives on this issue, *Teen Rights and Freedoms: Health Care* sheds light on the rights and freedoms of minors in making their own health care decisions.

Chronology

1944

In *Prince v. Massachusetts* the US Supreme Court asserts that parental authority is not absolute and the government has broad authority to regulate the actions and treatment of children.

1965

In *Griswold v. Connecticut* the Supreme Court first recognizes a right to privacy for married couples, finding a state law prohibiting the use of contraceptives unconstitutional.

1972

In *Eisenstadt v. Baird* the Supreme Court rules that the right to privacy protects the right of unmarried couples to use birth control.

1973

In *Roe v. Wade* the Supreme Court determines that the right to privacy protects the right of women to choose abortion in the first two trimesters of pregnancy.

1976

In Planned Parenthood of Central Missouri v. Danforth the Supreme Court holds that states may not require parental consent for a minor's abortion, striking down one of many abortion restrictions implemented by Missouri.

1977

In *Carey v. Population Services International* the Supreme Court rules that the rights to privacy and intimate association identified in *Griswold v. Connecticut* (1965) also extend to minors, protecting their right to access contraceptives.

1979   In *Parham v. J.R.* the Supreme Court determines that parents usually have the authority to make decisions for their children, including the decision to have the child committed to a psychiatric hospital.

1979   In *Bellotti v. Baird* the Supreme Court rules that parental consent for a minor's abortion can be required as long as the alternative for a judicial bypass granting permission is available.

1981   In *H.L. v. Matheson* the Supreme Court holds that a statute requiring parental notice of abortion when possible does not violate the constitutional rights of an immature, dependent minor.

1982   In *Akron v. Akron Center for Reproductive Health, Inc.* the Supreme Court determines, among other things, that it is unconstitutional for a state to determine that all minors under the age of fifteen are too immature to make an abortion decision without parental approval.

1987   In *Cardwell v. Bechtol* the Supreme Court of Tennessee finds that medical treatment may be provided without parental consent to mature minors—reasoning that comes to be known as the mature minor doctrine.

1988
In *Walker v. Superior Court* the California Supreme Court finds that a mother was rightfully charged with manslaughter for failing to treat the meningitis that killed her daughter.

1989
In *In re E.G.* the Supreme Court of Illinois finds that there is a constitutional basis for allowing certain mature minors to refuse medical treatment.

1990
In *Hodgson v. Minnesota* the Supreme Court holds that a two-parent notice requirement is unconstitutional, even with a judicial bypass procedure.

1991
In *State v. McKown* the Minnesota Supreme Court dismisses manslaughter charges against parents whose child died after they failed to obtain medical treatment due to religious beliefs.

1992
In *Hermanson v. State* the Supreme Court of Florida determines that parents who withheld medical treatment from their diabetic daughter because of religious beliefs were not culpable for her death due to a state law accommodating religion.

| 1992 | In *Belcher v. Charleston Area Med. Center* the Supreme Court of Appeals of West Virginia holds that a physician must obtain parental consent prior to medical treatment, but a mature minor's consent may sometimes override parents' wishes. |

| 2000 | In *Commonwealth v. Nixon*, the Supreme Court of Pennsylvania decides that the maturity of a minor and the minor's constitutional right to privacy do not protect parents from involuntary manslaughter charges for failing to seek medical treatment for their child. |

| 2013 | In *State v. Neumann* the Wisconsin Supreme Court determines that parents whose failure to provide medical care for their child causes the child's death are not immune from prosecution for homicide despite the existence of a treatment-through-prayer statute. |

> *"Minors who previously had no medical rights now found themselves in the position of making decisions about the most intimate medical procedures."*

Minors' Rights Regarding Health Care Have Expanded in Past Decades

Gale Encyclopedia of Everyday Law

In the following viewpoint, the author argues that over the past sixty years, the rights of minors to make decisions regarding their own health care without parental consent have expanded in several areas. The author writes that the general rule is that minors are not capable of providing informed consent for health care and that such consent must be granted by parents. However, the author notes that in the case of family planning—or contraception and abortion—the US Supreme Court has granted minors a right to privacy. The author also notes that in cases involving emergencies, sexual abuse, mental health, and sexually transmitted disease, minors are often granted an exception to the general rule. The author explains that emancipation laws and the mature minor doctrine also impact decisions about a minor's right to consent to health care without parental involvement.

Sixty years ago, the issue of medical treatment of minors—children under the age of 18—would never have been considered controversial. At that time, parental consent was required for almost any type of medical treatment, as it was required for any other situation involving children. Minors were simply not considered competent to make medical decisions.

The Debate Over Minors' Rights

However, the past 60 years have witnessed a gradual expansion of the rights of minors, and health care has been no exception. Minors who previously had no medical rights now found themselves in the position of making decisions about the most intimate medical procedures.

But the area of medical treatment of minors is still controversial, especially as it relates to certain procedures and conditions such as abortion and sexually transmitted diseases. Many states grant minors broad leeway to determine the course of their medical treatment, and others grant them very few rights. There is little agreement by either medical professionals or state lawmakers as to how far minor rights should go regarding medical treatment.

What is at issue in the debate over minor rights to medical treatment is a tension between the parental responsibilities toward the child, the immaturity and vulnerability of children, and the child's right to be emancipated from the decision of the parent. This tension has produced a patchwork of laws and makes it difficult to make any overriding statements about minor and parental rights in regard to medical treatment.

The Doctrine of Informed Consent

The crux of the debate over the treatment of minors is the doctrine of informed consent. A person must offer informed consent to any medical treatment given to them, or the physicians involved can risk legal liability. Informed consent has always been a crucial part of the doctor-patient relationship, and has been viewed by courts as a fundamental right.

The Dilemma About Minors' Consent for Health Care

On the one hand, it seems eminently reasonable that parents should have the right and responsibility to make health care decisions for their minor child. On the other hand, it may be more important for a young person to have access to confidential medical services than it is to require that parents be informed of their child's condition. Minors who are sexually active, pregnant, or infected with a sexually transmitted disease (STD) and those who abuse drugs or alcohol may avoid seeking care if they must involve their parents.

Heather Boonstra and Elizabeth Nash, Guttmacher Report on Public Policy, *August 2000.*

But in the case of children, the question is, can they offer informed consent, or does that informed consent have to be provided by their parents, who may be seen as more capable of making a knowledgeable decision on a subject as important as medical care. Beyond this simple question are an important set of underlying questions, pertaining, for example, to the age at which a child may become capable of informed consent, and whether there are certain procedures in which informed consent is more important than others.

In general, for most medical procedures, the parent or legal guardian of the minor still has to grant consent for the procedure to be performed. While the state can challenge a parent's decision to refuse medically necessary treatment and can in some cases win the authority to make medical decisions on behalf of the child, the minor cannot make his or her own medical decisions.

This general rule is virtually always the case regarding any sort of medical treatment before the minor enters their teenage years—no state or court has ever authorized minors younger than

12 to make any sort of medical decision for themselves. But after the minor becomes a teenager, states begin to digress in terms of the responsibility the minor can take for medical decisions. Exceptions have been carved out for various medical procedures that allow teenage minors to have final say in their medical care.

Minors' Rights to Family Planning

Twenty-five states and the District of Columbia have laws that explicitly give minors the authority to consent to contraceptive services, and twenty-seven states and the District of Columbia specifically allow pregnant minors to the obtain prenatal care and delivery services without parental consent or notification.

The Title X federal family planning program, which supports clinics that provide contraceptive service and other reproductive health care to minors on a confidential basis and without the need for parental consent or notification, has seen efforts made by Congress to require consent or notification before a minor receives these services. All of these efforts, the most recent in 1998, have failed.

Probably the most controversial area of family planning and minors is abortion. Two states—Connecticut and Maine—as well as the District of Columbia have laws that give minors the right to obtain abortions on their own. In contrast, 37 states as of 2012 had laws restricting minors' rights to obtain abortions by either requiring them to obtain the permission of one or both parents, or to notify one or both of them of the procedure. The rest of the states either had no laws regarding parental consent and notification and abortion or laws that are currently blocked from going into effect by the courts of the state.

The family planning area and its relation to minors has been a difficult one for the states to tackle because of several Supreme Court rulings that have ruled that minors do have a limited right of privacy in respect to family planning issues. The court has ruled that if states are going to restrict the right of minors to have an abortion, they have to provide an alternative to the requirement of parental consent, to allow the minor to show she is mature enough to make the decision of having an abortion herself. This alternative is generally in the form of a judicial bypass—permitting a court to make the decision regarding whether the minor can get an abortion. Maryland allows a "physician bypass" that permits a doctor to waive parental notice if the minor is capable of giving informed consent or if notice would lead to abuse of the minor.

Also, because of the Supreme Court rulings, states that do not explicitly allow minors to obtain contraceptive and prenatal care services without parental consent still must permit this to happen in practice, as the court has ruled that these are services that are covered by the minors' right to privacy. However, states can still impose limitations on minors' ability to obtain these services, based on factors such as age, marriage status, medical condition or who referred the minors for treatment. In addition, two states—Utah and Texas—prohibit the use of state funds to provide contraceptive services to minors without parental consent.

Other Exceptions to the General Rule

All states allow parental consent for treatment of a minor to be waived in the event of a medical emergency. The circumstances that should be present in order for such an emergency include the patient being incapacitated to the point of being unable to give an informed choice, the circumstances being life-threatening or serious enough that immediate treatment is required, and it being impossible or imprudent to try to get consent from someone regarding the patient. In these cases, consent of the parent is presumed, since otherwise the minor would suffer avoidable injury.

Most states allow minors to seek treatment for sexual abuse or assault without parental consent; however, many states require the minor's parents or guardian to be notified of the sexual abuse unless the physician has reason to believe the parent or guardian was responsible for the sexual abuse.

Planned Parenthood supporters participate in a rally on April 7, 2011, in Washington, DC. Federal funding for Planned Parenthood, which provides services for family planning, has become a contested issue in the United States. © Mark Wilson/Getty Images.

Twenty states and the District of Columbia give minors the explicit authority to consent to outpatient mental health services. No state specifically requires parental consent to obtain these services, but many states do impose age requirements or other restrictions in regards to minors who obtain these services.

Forty-four states and the District of Columbia have laws or policies authorizing a minor who abuses drug or alcohol to consent to outpatient counseling without a parent's consent. Again, no states require parental consent for these services, but some restrictions may be imposed on which minors can obtain this counseling.

Every state currently allows minors over the age of 12 to receive testing for sexually transmitted diseases, including HIV, without parental consent. Most of these states allow minors to receive treatment for all sexually transmitted diseases without parental consent. One state, Iowa, requires that parents be notified in the event of a positive HIV test. Many states allow doctors to notify the parents of the results of tests and treatment for sexually transmitted diseases, though they do not require the doctor to get consent.

The Impact of Emancipation

In addition to making exceptions to the general rule requiring informed consent for specific medical treatments, states will often allow minors to consent to medical treatment on the basis of their status—whether they are considered emancipated from their parents. Most states determine a child has reached the age of majority and is emancipated from his or her parents upon reaching the age of 18, although in Alabama and Nebraska, 19 is considered the age of majority, and in Pennsylvania it is 21. Mississippi sets the age of majority at 21, but 18 as the age of consent for health care decisions.

Beyond age, courts can declare a minor emancipated from their parents and thus able to issue consent, if they meet certain conditions, including self-sufficiency, living separate and apart from the parents, receiving money from a business activity not related to the parents, and proven capability of managing their own affairs. Married and divorced minors are often considered automatically emancipated, as are minors on active duty with the armed forces. In addition, minor parents are allowed to make medical decisions for their children. In 29 states and the District of Columbia, this consent is explicitly authorized.

The Mature Minor Doctrine

The "mature minor" doctrine provides for minors to give consent to medical procedures if they can show that they are mature enough to make a decision on their own. Only a few states such as Arkansas and Nevada have enacted the doctrine into statute. In several other states, including Pennsylvania, Tennessee, Illinois, Maine and Massachusetts, state high courts have adopted the doctrine as law.

In the states where it exists, the mature minor doctrine takes into account the age and situation of the minor to determine maturity, in addition to factors and conduct that can prove maturity. The Arkansas statute states, "any unemancipated minor of sufficient intelligence to understand and appreciate the consequences of the proposed surgical or medical treatment or procedures, for himself [may offer consent]." The standard is typical of the requirements of the mature minor doctrine.

The mature minor doctrine has been consistently applied in cases where the minor is 16 years or older, understands the medical procedure in question, and the procedure is not serious. Application of the doctrine in other circumstances is more questionable. Outside reproductive rights, the U.S. Supreme Court has never ruled on its applicability to medical procedures.

Confidentiality of Medical Records

States that allow minors to consent to certain medical procedures often provide for confidentiality from parents in regard to those medical procedures. However, this is not always the case. Many states allow the doctor to inform parents of medical procedures, and some states require parental notifications about specific medical procedures done on minors even when the minor has given consent.

When confidentiality is provided for, California's statute is typical of the requirements. It states that except as provided by law or if the minor authorizes it in writing, physicians are prohibited from telling the minor's parents or legal guardian about medical care the minor was legally able to authorize. The physician is required to discuss with the minor the advantages of disclosing the proposed treatment to the minor's parents or legal guardian before services are rendered.

> *"The right to privacy in connection with decisions affecting procreation extends to minors, as well as to adults."*

The Right to Privacy Protects a Minor's Right to Access Contraceptives

The Supreme Court's Decision

William J. Brennan Jr.

In the following viewpoint Justice William J. Brennan Jr., writing for the majority on the US Supreme Court, finds a New York law criminalizing the sale of birth control to minors unconstitutional. Brennan notes that the court has recognized a right to privacy in many areas, especially as such a right relates to reproduction. Brennan reasons that although the state may sometimes impose restrictions on minors that do not apply to adults, because of the court's previous decisions determining that the right to privacy protects the abortion rights of minors, it follows that restricting access to contraceptives also violates privacy rights. Brennan was an associate justice of the US Supreme Court from 1956 until his retirement in 1990.

William J. Brennan Jr., Majority opinion, *Carey v. Population Services International*, US Supreme Court, June 9, 1977.

Under New York Educ. Law § 6811(8), it is a crime (1) for any person to sell or distribute any contraceptive of any kind to a minor under the age of 16 years. . . .

The Right of Privacy

Although "[t]he Constitution does not explicitly mention any right of privacy," the Court has recognized that one aspect of the "liberty" protected by the Due Process Clause of the Fourteenth Amendment is "a right of personal privacy, or a guarantee of certain areas or zones of privacy" [*Roe v. Wade* (1973)]. This right of personal privacy includes "the interest in independence in making certain kinds of important decisions." This right of personal privacy includes "the interest in independence in making certain kinds of important decisions" [*Whalen v. Roe,* (1977)]. While the outer limits of this aspect of privacy have not been marked by the Court, it is clear that among the decisions that an individual may make without unjustified government interference are personal decisions

> relating to marriage, procreation, contraception, family relationships, and childrearing and education.

The decision whether or not to beget or bear a child is at the very heart of this cluster of constitutionally protected choices. That decision holds a particularly important place in the history of the right of privacy, a right first explicitly recognized in an opinion holding unconstitutional a statute prohibiting the use of contraceptives, and most prominently vindicated in recent years in the contexts of contraception and abortion. This is understandable, for in a field that, by definition, concerns the most intimate of human activities and relationships, decisions whether to accomplish or to prevent conception are among the most private and sensitive.

> If the right of privacy means anything, it is the right of the individual, married or single, to be free of unwarranted governmental intrusion into matters so fundamentally affecting a person as the decision whether to bear or beget a child. [*Eisenstadt v. Baird* (1972).]

Jose Ramirez, of La Clínica del Pueblo, discusses safe sex with teens in Washington, DC. In Carey v. Population Services International *(1977), the US Supreme Court granted minors the right to obtain contraceptives.* © Nikki Kahn/The Washington Post/Getty Images.

That the constitutionally protected right of privacy extends to an individual's liberty to make choices regarding contraception does not, however, automatically invalidate every state regulation in this area. The business of manufacturing and selling contraceptives may be regulated in ways that do not infringe protected individual choices. And even a burdensome regulation may be validated by a sufficiently compelling state interest. In *Roe v. Wade*, for example, after determining that the "right of privacy . . . encompass[es] a woman's decision whether or not to terminate her pregnancy," we cautioned that the right is not absolute, and that certain state interests (in that case, "interests in safeguarding health, in maintaining medical standards, and in protecting potential life") may at some point "become sufficiently compelling to sustain regulation of the factors that govern the abortion decision." "Compelling" is of course the key word; where a decision as fundamental as that whether to bear or beget a child is involved, regulations imposing a burden on it may be justified only by compelling state interests, and must be narrowly drawn to express only those interests. . . .

The Constitutional Rights of Minors

The question of the extent of state power to regulate conduct of minors not constitutionally regulable when committed by adults is a vexing one, perhaps not susceptible of precise answer. We have been reluctant to attempt to define "the totality of the relationship of the juvenile and the state" [*In re Gault* (1967)]. Certain principles, however, have been recognized. "Minors, as well as adults, are protected by the Constitution, and possess constitutional rights" [*Planned Parenthood of Central Missouri v. Danforth* (1976)]. "[W]hatever may be their precise impact, neither the Fourteenth Amendment nor the Bill of Rights is for adults alone" [*In re Gault*]. On the other hand, we have held in a variety of contexts that "the power of the state to control the conduct of children reaches beyond the scope of its authority over adults" [*Prince v. Massachusetts* (1944)].

Of particular significance to the decision of this case, the right to privacy in connection with decisions affecting procreation extends to minors, as well as to adults. *Planned Parenthood of Central Missouri v. Danforth*, held that a State

> may not impose a blanket provision . . . requiring the consent of a parent or person *in loco parentis* [in the place of a parent] as a condition for abortion of an unmarried minor during the first 12 weeks of her pregnancy.

As in the case of the spousal consent requirement struck down in the same case, "the State does not have the constitutional authority to give a third party an absolute, and possibly arbitrary, veto," "'which the state itself is absolutely and totally prohibited from exercising.'" State restrictions inhibiting privacy rights of minors are valid only if they serve "any significant state interest . . . that is not present in the case of an adult." *Planned Parenthood* found that no such interest justified a state requirement of parental consent.

Since the State may not impose a blanket prohibition, or even a blanket requirement of parental consent, on the choice of a minor to terminate her pregnancy, the constitutionality of a blanket prohibition of the distribution of contraceptives to minors is *a fortiori* [with greater reason] foreclosed. The State's interests in protection of the mental and physical health of the pregnant minor, and in protection of potential life are clearly more implicated by the abortion decision than by the decision to use a nonhazardous contraceptive.

The State's Interest in Deterring Teenage Sex

Appellants argue, however, that significant state interests are served by restricting minors' access to contraceptives, because free availability to minors of contraceptives would lead to increased sexual activity among the young, in violation of the policy of New York to discourage such behavior. The argument is that minors' sexual activity may be deterred by increasing the hazards attendant on it. The same argument, however, would support a ban on abortions for minors, or indeed support a prohibition on abortions, or access to contraceptives, for the unmarried, whose sexual activity is also against the public policy of many State[s]. Yet, in each of these areas, the Court has rejected the argument, noting in *Roe v. Wade* that "no court or commentator has taken the argument seriously." The reason for this unanimous rejection was stated in *Eisenstadt v. Baird*:

> It would be plainly unreasonable to assume that [the State] has prescribed pregnancy and the birth of an unwanted child [or the physical and psychological dangers of an abortion] as punishment for fornication.

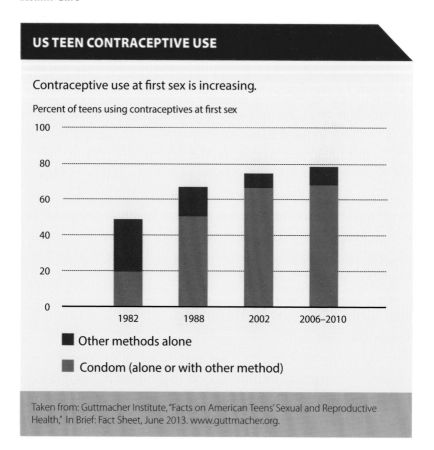

US TEEN CONTRACEPTIVE USE

Contraceptive use at first sex is increasing.

Percent of teens using contraceptives at first sex

■ Other methods alone

■ Condom (alone or with other method)

Taken from: Guttmacher Institute, "Facts on American Teens' Sexual and Reproductive Health," In Brief: Fact Sheet, June 2013. www.guttmacher.org.

We remain reluctant to attribute any such "scheme of values" to the State.

Moreover, there is substantial reason for doubt whether limiting access to contraceptives will, in fact, substantially discourage early sexual behavior. Appellants themselves conceded in the District Court that "there is no evidence that teenage extramarital sexual activity increases in proportion to the availability of contraceptives," and accordingly offered none, in the District Court or here. Appellees, on the other hand, cite a considerable body of evidence and opinion indicating that there is no such deterrent effect. Although we take judicial notice, as did the District Court, that with or without access to contraceptives, the incidence of sexual activity among minors is high, and the consequence of such activity are frequently devastating, the studies cited by appellees play no part in our decision. It is enough that we again confirm the principle that, when a State, as here, burdens the exercise of a fundamental right, its attempt to justify that burden as a rational means for the accomplishment of some significant state policy requires more than a bare assertion, based on a conceded complete absence of supporting evidence, that the burden is connected to such a policy.

Appellants argue that New York does not totally prohibit distribution of contraceptives to minors under 16, and that, accordingly, § 611(8) cannot be held unconstitutional. Although § 6811(8), on its face, is a flat unqualified prohibition, Educ. Law § 6807(b) provides that nothing in Education Law §§ 6800-6826 shall be construed to prevent "[a]ny physician . . . from supplying his patients with such drugs as [he] . . . deems proper in connection with his practice." This narrow exception, however, does not save the statute. As we have held above as to limitations upon distribution to adults, less than total restrictions on access to contraceptives that significantly burden the right to decide whether to bear children must also pass constitutional scrutiny. Appellants assert no medical necessity for imposing a medical limitation on the distribution of nonprescription contraceptives to minors. Rather, they argue that such a restriction serves to emphasize to young people the seriousness with which the State views the decision to engage in sexual intercourse at an early age. But this is only another form of the argument that juvenile sexual conduct will be deterred by making contraceptives more difficult to obtain. Moreover, that argument is particularly poorly suited to the restriction appellants are attempting to justify, which on appellants' construction delegates the State's authority to disapprove of minors' sexual behavior to physicians, who may exercise it arbitrarily, either to deny contraceptives to young people, or to undermine the State's policy of discouraging illicit early sexual behavior. This the State may not do.

"If the State decides to require a
pregnant minor to obtain one or both
parents' consent to an abortion, it also
must provide an alternative procedure
whereby authorization for the abortion
can be obtained."

Parental Consent for a Minor's Abortion Cannot Be Absolute

The Supreme Court's Decision

Lewis F. Powell Jr.

In the following viewpoint, Justice Lewis F. Powell Jr., writing for a plurality of the US Supreme Court, finds that states may require parental consent in order for a minor to get an abortion as long as the state provides an alternative procedure for the minor to obtain permission. Powell notes that the court's previous decisions support the unique treatment of minors under the law, including respect for the role of parents. Powell notes that the court determined in Planned Parenthood of Central Missouri v. Danforth *(1976) that the state may not require parental consent with no alternatives, but he concludes states may require parental consent as long as they allow the possibility for anonymous and quick judicial authorization as well. Powell was an associate justice on the US Supreme Court from 1972 until 1987.*

Lewis F. Powell Jr., Plurality opinion, *Bellotti v. Baird*, US Supreme Court, July 2, 1979.

A child, merely on account of his minority, is not beyond the protection of the Constitution. As the Court said in *In re Gault*, "whatever may be their precise impact, neither the Fourteenth Amendment nor the Bill of Rights is for adults alone." This observation, of course, is but the beginning of the analysis. The Court long has recognized that the status of minors under the law is unique in many respects. As Mr. Justice [Felix] Frankfurter aptly put it: "Children have a very special place in life which law should reflect. Legal theories and their phrasing in other cases readily lead to fallacious reasoning if uncritically transferred to determination of a State's duty towards children" [*May v. Anderson* (1953) (concurring opinion)]. The unique role in our society of the family, the institution by which "we inculcate and pass down many of our most cherished values, moral and cultural" [*Moore v. East Cleveland* (1977) (plurality opinion)], requires that constitutional principles be applied with sensitivity and flexibility to the special needs of parents and children. We have recognized three reasons justifying the conclusion that the constitutional rights of children cannot be equated with those of adults: the peculiar vulnerability of children; their inability to make critical decisions in an informed, mature manner; and the importance of the parental role in child rearing.

The Constitutional Rights of Children

The Court's concern for the vulnerability of children is demonstrated in its decisions dealing with minors' claims to constitutional protection against deprivations of liberty or property interests by the State. With respect to many of these claims, we have concluded that the child's right is virtually coextensive with that of an adult. For example, the Court has held that the Fourteenth Amendment's guarantee against the deprivation of liberty without due process of law is applicable to children in juvenile delinquency proceedings. In particular, minors involved in such proceedings are entitled to adequate notice, the assistance of counsel, and the opportunity to confront their accusers.

They can be found guilty only upon proof beyond a reasonable doubt, and they may assert the privilege against compulsory self-incrimination. Similarly, in *Goss v. Lopez* (1975), the Court held that children may not be deprived of certain property interests without due process.

These rulings have not been made on the uncritical assumption that the constitutional rights of children are indistinguishable from those of adults. Indeed, our acceptance of juvenile courts distinct from the adult criminal justice system assumes that juvenile offenders constitutionally may be treated differently from adults. In order to preserve this separate avenue for dealing with minors, the Court has said that hearings in juvenile delinquency cases need not necessarily "'conform with all of the requirements of a criminal trial or even of the usual administrative hearing'" [*In re Gault*, quoting *Kent v. United States* (1966)]. Thus, juveniles are not constitutionally entitled to trial by jury in delinquency adjudications. Viewed together, our cases show that although children generally are protected by the same constitutional guarantees against governmental deprivations as are adults, the State is entitled to adjust its legal system to account for children's vulnerability and their needs for "concern, . . . sympathy, and . . . paternal attention" [*McKeiver v. Pennsylvania* (1971) (plurality opinion)].

Limits on Children's Rights

Second, the Court has held that the States validly may limit the freedom of children to choose for themselves in the making of important, affirmative choices with potentially serious consequences. These rulings have been grounded in the recognition that, during the formative years of childhood and adolescence, minors often lack the experience, perspective, and judgment to recognize and avoid choices that could be detrimental to them.

Ginsberg v. New York (1968), illustrates well the Court's concern over the inability of children to make mature choices, as the First Amendment rights involved are clear examples of

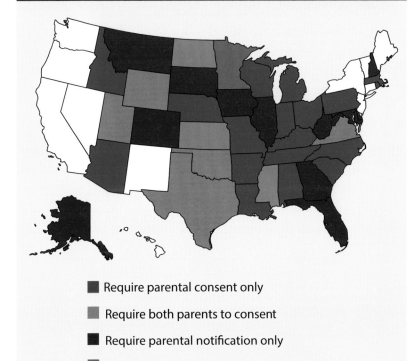

PARENTAL INVOLVEMENT LAWS AS OF OCTOBER 2013

■ Require parental consent only

■ Require both parents to consent

■ Require parental notification only

■ Require that both parents be notified

■ Require both parental consent and notification

Taken from: Guttmacher Institute, "Parental Involvement in Minors' Abortions," *State Policies in Brief*, October 1, 2013. www.guttmacher.org.

constitutionally protected freedoms of choice. At issue was a criminal conviction for selling sexually oriented magazines to a minor under the age of 17 in violation of a New York state law. It was conceded that the conviction could not have stood under the First Amendment if based upon a sale of the same material to an adult. Notwithstanding the importance the Court always has attached to First Amendment rights, it concluded that "even where there is an invasion of protected freedoms 'the power of the state to control the conduct of children reaches beyond the scope of its authority over adults . . . ,'" [quoting *Prince v. Massachusetts* (1944)]. The Court was convinced that the New York Legislature rationally could conclude that the sale to children of the magazines in question presented a danger against which they should be guarded. It therefore rejected the argument that the New York law violated the constitutional rights of minors.

The Role of Parents

Third, the guiding role of parents in the upbringing of their children justifies limitations on the freedoms of minors. The State commonly protects its youth from adverse governmental action and from their own immaturity by requiring parental consent to or involvement in important decisions by minors. But an additional and more important justification for state deference to parental control over children is that "[t]he child is not the mere creature of the State; those who nurture him and direct his destiny have the right, coupled with the high duty, to recognize and prepare him for additional obligations" [*Pierce v. Society of Sisters* (1925)]. "The duty to prepare the child for 'additional obligations' . . . must be read to include the inculcation of moral standards, religious beliefs, and elements of good citizenship" [*Wisconsin v. Yoder* (1972)]. This affirmative process of teaching, guiding, and inspiring by precept and example is essential to the growth of young people into mature, socially responsible citizens.

We have believed in this country that this process, in large part, is beyond the competence of impersonal political institutions. Indeed, affirmative sponsorship of particular ethical, religious, or political beliefs is something we expect the State not to attempt in a society constitutionally committed to the ideal of individual liberty and freedom of choice. Thus, "[i]t is cardinal with us that the custody, care and nurture of the child reside first in the parents, whose primary function and freedom include preparation for obligations the state can neither supply nor hinder" [*Prince v. Massachusetts*].

Unquestionably, there are many competing theories about the most effective way for parents to fulfill their central role in assisting their children on the way to responsible adulthood. While we do not pretend any special wisdom on this subject, we cannot ignore that central to many of these theories, and deeply rooted in our Nation's history and tradition, is the belief that the parental role implies a substantial measure of authority over one's children. Indeed, "constitutional interpretation has consistently recognized that the parents' claim to authority in their own household to direct the rearing of their children is basic in the structure of our society" [*Ginsberg v. New York*].

Properly understood, then, the tradition of parental authority is not inconsistent with our tradition of individual liberty; rather, the former is one of the basic presuppositions of the latter. Legal restrictions on minors, especially those supportive of the parental role, may be important to the child's chances for the full growth and maturity that make eventual participation in a free society meaningful and rewarding. Under the Constitution, the State can "properly conclude that parents and others, teachers for example, who have [the] primary responsibility for children's well-being are entitled to the support of laws designed to aid discharge of that responsibility" [*Ginsberg v. New York*]. . . .

Parental Involvement in Abortion

As immature minors often lack the ability to make fully informed choices that take account of both immediate and long-range consequences, a State reasonably may determine that parental consultation often is desirable and in the best interest of the minor. It may further determine, as a general proposition, that such consultation is particularly desirable with respect to the abortion decision—one that for some people raises profound moral and religious concerns. As Mr. Justice [Potter] Stewart wrote in concurrence in *Planned Parenthood of Central Missouri v. Danforth* [1976]:

In 2005 Arkansas governor Mike Huckabee signed a bill into law requiring parental notification for minors to have an abortion. In Bellotti v. Baird *(1979), the US Supreme Court ruled that states may require parental consent for an abortion as long as they grant minors the ability to receive judicial authorization as well.* © Danny Johnston/Associated Press.

There can be little doubt that the State furthers a constitutionally permissible end by encouraging an unmarried pregnant minor to seek the help and advice of her parents in making the very important decision whether or not to bear a child. That is a grave decision, and a girl of tender years, under emotional stress, may be ill-equipped to make it without mature advice and emotional support. It seems unlikely that she will obtain adequate counsel and support from the attending physician at an abortion clinic, where abortions for pregnant minors frequently take place.

But we are concerned here with a constitutional right to seek an abortion. The abortion decision differs in important ways from other decisions that may be made during minority. The need to preserve the constitutional right and the unique nature of the abortion decision, especially when made by a minor, require a State to act with particular sensitivity when it legislates to foster parental involvement in this matter.

The Need to Avoid Absolute Veto

The pregnant minor's options are much different from those facing a minor in other situations, such as deciding whether to marry. A minor not permitted to marry before the age of majority is required simply to postpone her decision. She and her intended spouse may preserve the opportunity for later marriage should they continue to desire it. A pregnant adolescent, however, cannot preserve for long the possibility of aborting, which effectively expires in a matter of weeks from the onset of pregnancy.

Moreover, the potentially severe detriment facing a pregnant woman is not mitigated by her minority. Indeed, considering her probable education, employment skills, financial resources, and emotional maturity, unwanted motherhood may be exceptionally burdensome for a minor. In addition, the fact of having a child brings with it adult legal responsibility, for parenthood, like attainment of the age of majority, is one of the traditional criteria for the termination of the legal disabilities of minority. In sum, there are few situations in which denying a minor the right to make an important decision will have consequences so grave and indelible.

Yet, an abortion may not be the best choice for the minor. The circumstances in which this issue arises will vary widely. In a given case, alternatives to abortion, such as marriage to the father of the child, arranging for its adoption, or assuming the responsibilities of motherhood with the assured support of family, may be feasible and relevant to the minor's best interests. Nonetheless, the abortion decision is one that simply cannot be postponed, or it will be made by default with far-reaching consequences.

For these reasons, as we held in *Planned Parenthood of Central Missouri v. Danforth*, "the State may not impose a blanket provision . . . requiring the consent of a parent or person *in loco parentis* [acting in the place of a parent] as a condition for abortion of an unmarried minor during the first 12 weeks of her pregnancy." Although such deference to parents may be permissible with respect to other choices facing a minor, the unique nature and consequences of the abortion decision make it inappropriate "to give a third party an absolute, and possibly arbitrary, veto over the decision of the physician and his patient to terminate the patient's pregnancy, regardless of the reason for withholding the consent." We therefore conclude that if the State decides to require a pregnant minor to obtain one or both parents' consent to an abortion, it also must provide an alternative procedure whereby authorization for the abortion can be obtained.

A pregnant minor is entitled in such a proceeding to show either: (1) that she is mature enough and well enough informed to make her abortion decision, in consultation with her physician, independently of her parents' wishes; (2) that even if she is not able to make this decision independently, the desired abortion would be in her best interests. The proceeding in which this showing is made must assure that a resolution of the issue, and any appeals that may follow, will be completed with anonymity and sufficient expedition to provide an effective opportunity for an abortion to be obtained. In sum, the procedure must ensure that the provision requiring parental consent does not in fact amount to the "absolute, and possibly arbitrary, veto" that was found impermissible in *Danforth*.

> *"Parental consent laws boast a 71 percent nationwide approval rating, protect the health and well-being of minors, respect parental rights, and save the lives of unborn babies."*

Parental Involvement Laws for Abortion Protect Minors and Parents

Mary E. Harned

In the following viewpoint Mary E. Harned argues that parental involvement laws for abortion—both parental notification laws and parental consent laws—protect the health and safety of minors, uphold the rights of parents, and save the lives of unborn babies. Harned contends that current parental notification laws could benefit from better enforcement and more stringent requirements. She argues that clarification is needed for courts in assessing a minor's maturity level, should a minor use the courts to attempt to bypass the parental involvement requirement. Harned is staff counsel for Americans United for Life, a nonprofit law and policy organization that works to protect life under the law.

In 2011, Connecticut—one of only 12 states without a law requiring parental consent or notification before a minor may obtain an abortion—drew national attention when legislative consideration of a bill that would require parental consent for the use of tanning parlors evolved into an abortion debate. One brave legislator confronted his colleagues with a disturbing fact: while the state requires parental consent for tattooing and body piercing, and intended to extend that requirement to the use of tanning parlors, minors may obtain an abortion in Connecticut without any parental involvement. However, when the state senator tried to add a provision requiring parental consent for abortion to the bill, the legislature abandoned it altogether.

The Benefits of Parental Involvement Laws

It is difficult to comprehend the Connecticut legislature's strong opposition to a law requiring parental consent prior to a minors abortion, when parental consent laws boast a 71 percent nationwide approval rating, protect the health and well-being of minors, respect parental rights, and save the lives of unborn babies. In fact, this popular legislation saw a rebirth in 2011, with at least 24 states considering one or more measures to enact new or strengthen existing consent or notification requirements.

Why the interest in and support for these laws? The medical, emotional, and psychological consequences of abortion are often serious and can be lasting, particularly when the patient is immature. Moreover, parents usually possess information essential to a physician's exercise of his or her best medical judgment concerning the minor. Parents who are aware that their daughter has had an abortion may better ensure the best post-abortion medical attention. Further, minors who obtain "secret" abortions often do so at the behest of the older men who impregnated them, and then return to abusive situations. News stories frequently reveal yet another teen that has been sexually abused by a person in authority—a coach, teacher, or other authority figure. Every day, teens are taken to abortion clinics without the consent or even the knowledge of their parents. Minors are at risk in every state in which parental involvement laws have not been enacted or are easily circumvented.

In addition, parental involvement laws save the lives of unborn babies by reducing the demand for abortions by minors. For example, a 1996 study [according to D. Haas-Wilson] revealed that "parental involvement laws appear to decrease minors' demands for abortion by 13 to 25 percent." A 2008 study showed that parental consent laws reduce the minor abortion rate by 18.7 percent. With the loving support of their parents, many young women are able to bring their babies into the world and not face the physical risks and emotional devastation that abortions can bring.

The Courts' Decisions on Parental Involvement

The U.S. Supreme Court has reviewed statutes requiring parental consent or notification before a minor may obtain an abortion on 11 different occasions. The Court's decisions in these cases provide state legislators with concrete guidelines on how to draft parental involvement laws that will be upheld by the courts.

Based upon Supreme Court precedent and subsequent lower federal court decisions, a parental involvement law is constitutional and does not place an undue burden on minors if it contains the following provisions:

For consent, no physician may perform an abortion upon a minor or incompetent person unless the physician has the consent of one parent or legal guardian. For notice, no physician may perform an abortion upon a minor or incompetent person unless the physician performing the abortion has given 48 hours notice to a parent or legal guardian of the minor or incompetent person.

An exception to the consent or notice requirement exists when there is a medical emergency or when notice is waived by the person entitled to receive the notice.

In 1989 antiabortion demonstrators rally in Tallahassee, Florida, after the State Supreme Court ruled that minors have the right to seek abortions without parental consent. By 2013 twelve states did not require parental consent or notification before a minor may obtain an abortion. © Bettmann/Corbis.

A minor may bypass the requirement through the courts (i.e., judicial waiver or bypass).

AUL [Americans United for Life] has drafted both a model "Parental Consent for Abortion Act" as well as a "Parental Notification of Abortion Act," which are based upon Supreme Court precedent and take these issues into consideration.

The Requirement of Judicial Bypass

In *Bellotti v. Baird (Bellotti II)* [1979], the Court held that a state which requires a pregnant minor to obtain one or both parents' consent to an abortion must "provide an alternative procedure whereby authorization for the abortion can be obtained." This procedure must include the following four elements:

- An allowance for the minor to show that "she is mature enough and well enough informed to make her abortion decision, in consultation with her physician, independently of her parents' wishes";
- An allowance for the minor to alternatively show that "even if she is not able to make this decision independently, the desired abortion would be in her best interests";
- The proceedings in which one of these showings is made must be "completed with anonymity"; and
- The proceedings in which one of these showings is made must be "completed with . . . sufficient expedition to provide an effective opportunity for an abortion to be obtained."

In *Ohio v. Akron Center for Reproductive Health (Akron II)* [1990], the Court left open the question of whether a statute requiring parental notice rather than consent required bypass procedures. The Court stated that given "the greater intrusiveness of consent statutes . . . a bypass procedure that will suffice for a consent statute will suffice also for a notice statute." In other words, when a state includes in its parental notification law bypass procedures that meet the constitutional requirements for a consent bypass, the state's bypass procedures are unquestionably constitutional.

The Medical Emergency Exception

In the 1992 case *Planned Parenthood v. Casey*, a plurality of the United States Supreme Court reaffirmed that a state may constitutionally "require a minor seeking an abortion to obtain the consent of a parent or guardian, provided that there is an adequate judicial bypass procedure." The Court further held that an exception to the parental consent requirement for a "medical emergency" was sufficient to protect a minor's health, and imposed "no undue burden" on her access to abortion.

The Supreme Court noted that the Court of Appeals construed the phrase "serious risk" in the definition of "medical emergency" to include serious conditions that would affect the health of the minor. The lower court stated, "We read the medical emergency exception as intended by the Pennsylvania legislature to assure that compliance with its abortion regulations would not in any way pose a significant threat to the life or health of a woman." Based on this reading, the Court in *Casey* held that the medical emergency definition "imposes no undue burden on a woman's abortion right."

Tragically, it is often easy for abortion providers to sidestep a law requiring parental consent or notice by claiming they were "duped" into accepting consent from or providing notice to individuals fraudulently representing themselves as the parents or guardians of minors. Other potential loopholes in parental consent or notice statutes include: the inappropriate use of an emergency exception by an abortion provider; exploitation of the judicial bypass system through "forum shopping" (finding courts likely to grant a judicial bypass); a low burden of proof for a minor to show that she is mature enough to make her own abortion decision, or that parental consent or notice is not in her best interest; and a lack of guidance to courts on how to evaluate a minor's maturity or what is in her best interest.

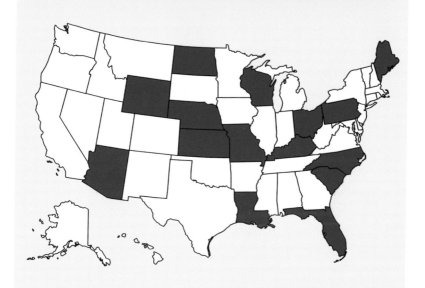

PARENTAL INVOLVEMENT ENHANCEMENTS: JUDICIAL BYPASS STANDARDS

At least fifteen states provide standards for judges to use when considering the "maturity" and/or "best interests of minors" in judicial bypass proceedings: AZ, FL, KS, KY, LA, ME, MO, NE, NC, ND, OH, PA, SC, WI, and WY.

Taken from: Mary E. Harned, "Parental Involvement Laws: Protecting Minors and Parental Rights," *Defending Life 2013*. Washington, DC: Americans United for Life, 2013. www.aul.org.

To assist states in better protecting minors and parental rights, AUL has drafted the "Parental Involvement Enhancement Act" to reinforce existing parental involvement laws with the enhancements discussed below.

Suggested Enhancements to Parental Involvement Laws

In parental consent states, a consenting parent or guardian should be required to present government-issued identification before a minor obtains an abortion. In parental notice states, a parent or guardian should be required to present identification when waiving the right to notice. In addition to providing identification, a parent or guardian should provide documentation proving that they are the parent or legal guardian of the minor seeking an abortion. Copies of the identification and proof of relationship must then be kept by the abortion clinic in the minor's medical records. When such actions are required, ignorance of an adult's true identity is not an excuse for failing to follow the law.

Another method states may utilize to ensure that the appropriate person is providing consent or waiving notice is to require the notarization of the applicable form(s). Like the identification and proof of relationship requirements discussed above, notarization requirements help ensure that the correct person has consented or has been notified of plans to perform an abortion on a minor. Further, it is difficult for abortion providers to subvert this requirement.

A "medical emergency" exception in parental involvement laws should not be a license for abortion providers to circumvent the law. Further, a minor who has an abortion following a medical emergency will often require more follow-up care and support from her parents or guardians. Therefore, states can ensure that parental involvement laws are not circumvented and that minors are better protected by requiring abortion providers to promptly notify a parent or guardian that a minor had an "emergency" abortion, the reason for the abortion, and a description of necessary follow-up care.

Some judges or courts are more inclined to grant judicial waiver requests than others. Undoubtedly, abortion providers know which judges or courts are "friendly" to subverting parental rights, and may guide minors to seek a bypass in those courts. To prevent this and better protect minors, states may require a minor to seek a bypass in a court of jurisdiction within her home county.

Suggested Enhancements to Judicial Bypass

States may require courts to find "clear and convincing evidence"—evidence showing a high probability of truth of the factual matter at issue—that a minor is either: 1) sufficiently mature and well-informed to consent to an abortion without parental involvement; or 2) that an abortion without parental involvement is in her best interest. "Clear and convincing evidence" is an intermediate standard of proof—higher than "preponderance of the evidence" (more likely than not), but lower than "beyond a reasonable doubt" (used in criminal cases). While judges have broad discretion under most parental involvement laws (their decision to grant a bypass is not subject to review), the "clear and convincing evidence" standard better ensures that judges carefully examine and weigh the facts presented to them in bypass proceedings.

Courts benefit from the provision of specific standards for judicial review in evaluating judicial bypass petitions. Currently, most consent and notice requirements contain very basic criteria, simply requiring that the minor be mature enough to make the decision, or requiring that the abortion be in the minor's "best interest."

An Arizona appellate court case [*In the Matter of B.S.* (Ariz. Ct. App. 2003)] delineated criteria that a judge should use in evaluating the maturity of a minor petitioning for judicial bypass. Specifically, the court's decision:

- Endorsed an examination of the minor's "experience, perspective, and judgment"; Defined "experience" as "all that has happened to the minor in her lifetime including things she has seen or done";

- Provided that, in assessing a minor's experience level, the court should consider such things as the minor's age and experiences working outside the home, living away from home, handling personal finances, and making other "significant decisions";

- Defined "perspective," in the context of an abortion decision as the "minor's ability to appreciate and understand the relative gravity and possible detrimental impact of available options, as well as the potential consequences of each";
- Recommended that, in assessing a minor's perspective on her abortion decision, the court should examine the steps she took to explore her options and the extent to which she considered and weighed the potential consequences of each option;
- Defined "judgment" as the "minor's intellectual and emotional ability to make the abortion decision without the [involvement] of her parents or guardians";
- Provided that, in assessing judgment, the court should examine the minor's conduct since learning of her pregnancy and her intellectual ability to understand her options and make an informed decision.

This decision provides an excellent example of how, based upon Supreme Court precedent, the more basic judicial bypass requirements can be enhanced.

To further assist courts with their evaluation, states may permit a court to refer a minor for a mental health evaluation. This type of measure protects minors from their own immaturity or from coercion or abuse by others.

"*I personally have assisted more than a thousand minors who have called our 24/7 hotline in search of help to terminate a pregnancy.*"

A Hotline Director Explains Why She Helps Minors Obtain Abortions

Personal Narrative

Tina Hester

In the following viewpoint, Tina Hester explains that she helps young women in Texas navigate the legal process for seeking judicial bypass of the parental involvement required in that state for a minor's abortion. Hester claims that a recent Texas law only makes things more difficult for teenage girls seeking abortion, as it will reduce the number of abortion clinics. She argues that politicians are out of touch with the realities of young pregnant women. Hester is executive director of Jane's Due Process, a nonprofit organization that provides legal representation to pregnant teens, especially those seeking legal exceptions to parental involvement laws prior to terminating their pregnancies.

On Thursday [July 18, 2013], when Texas Gov. Rick Perry signed into law a sweeping abortion measure, my heart broke for all of what my Republican uncle in Lubbock calls "my girls." "My girls" are Texas minors seeking to terminate a pregnancy through the judicial bypass process. For the past six years, I have managed a legal hotline called Jane's Due Process. Primarily, we help minors from across Texas navigate the obstacle course known as the Texas judicial bypass law—or Chapter 33 cases, as our referral attorneys call them. I personally have assisted more than a thousand minors who have called our 24/7 hotline in search of help to terminate a pregnancy.

New Legislation in Texas

I have heard so many stories of abandonment, threats of being kicked out, threats of physical harm or harm to the boyfriends, families breaking up or falling on hard times, and parents with life-threatening diseases. Stories that burn into your psyche and spur bubbling rage when you hear Texas legislators callously decide to make rape or incest victims carry pregnancies to term, or close all but five of the roughly 40 abortion clinics in Texas. Basically, the bill would wipe out all abortion providers west of Interstate 35.

At the bill's signing, Gov. Perry was praised by state Rep. Jodie Laubenberg (R-Parker), the sponsor of the anti-abortion bill, known as HB 2. Laubenberg became an overnight sensation when during a debate on the bill she said, "In the emergency room they have what's called rape kits, where a woman can get cleaned out." Laubenberg said Perry would be known for "eternity" for his work.

Yet, all I can think about is the here and now—how to set up a transportation line to get minors, as well as all others seeking abortions—to a clinic that will survive the draconian targeted regulation of abortion provider (TRAP) laws.

The Realities of Pregnant Minors

When Gov. Perry signed HB 2, my heart especially broke for one girl and one baby. I picked up a minor this month to get her to court for a judicial bypass case. She is taking care of a baby she had nine months ago, a preemie who spent months in the neonatal unit and needs around-the-clock care. This minor has not left her house for months. She is in constant fear the Medicaid-provided nurses will screw up her baby's tracheostomy. As is true with so many of my cases, this minor was kicked off Medicaid 90 days after her delivery and thus was not eligible for state-funded family planning services. Texas has the highest rate of repeat teen births in the country and one of the highest teen pregnancy rates. This girl had the doubly bad luck to have a dad incarcerated for drug dealing and a mom suffering from schizophrenia. She has no family on which to fall back. She is alone. She would like to graduate from high school and go on to nursing school, but she is scared that being away from her house could allow undue harm to her baby.

As I watched the healthy and prosperous politicians at the bill signing, I couldn't help but think they live in a parallel universe far different from that of the minors who call our hotline. One in four of our clients is an orphan or orphan de facto. One in five of our clients already has been pregnant at least once, which is not really surprising because Texas' family planning network has been dismantled, and parental consent is required at many of the clinics that remain open.

It is for those reasons I ask Gov. Perry, Rep. Laubenberg, and anyone else who wants to outlaw abortion: Where are you when desperate folks are in desperate situations? Will you be there to remove the tracheostomy tube and clean the stoma? Will you make sure it is "cleaned out" so my girls can finish their education? Won't you lavish some of your compassion on my girls?

> *"Our precedents permit the parents to retain a substantial, if not the dominant, role in the decision, absent a finding of neglect or abuse, and that the traditional presumption that the parents act in the best interests of their child should apply."*

Commitment of Minors for Psychiatric Care Does Not Violate Due Process

The Supreme Court's Decision

Warren E. Burger

In the following viewpoint, Justice Warren E. Burger, writing for the majority on the US Supreme Court, finds that a Georgia law allowing voluntary commitment of minors to a mental hospital by their parents does not violate the due process rights of minors. Burger notes that although minors have a liberty interest in not being confined for medical treatment, the State has an interest in mental health and parents have an interest in the well-being of their children, both of which override the liberty interests of minors. Burger writes that as long as certain procedures are followed that ensure the neutrality of the decision to commit a minor, parental consent and physician approval override any disagreement a minor may have to commitment in a psychiatric institution. Burger was chief justice of the US Supreme Court from 1969 until his retirement in 1986.

Warren E. Burger, Majority opinion, *Parham v. J.R.*, US Supreme Court, June 29, 1979.

In an earlier day, the problems inherent in coping with children afflicted with mental or emotional abnormalities were dealt with largely within the family. Sometimes parents were aided by teachers or a family doctor. While some parents no doubt were able to deal with their disturbed children without specialized assistance, others, especially those of limited means and education, were not. Increasingly, they turned for assistance to local, public sources or private charities. Until recently, most of the states did little more than provide custodial institutions for the confinement of persons who were considered dangerous.

State Procedures and Due Process

As medical knowledge about the mentally ill and public concern for their condition expanded, the states, aided substantially by federal grants, have sought to ameliorate the human tragedies of seriously disturbed children. Ironically, as most states have expanded their efforts to assist the mentally ill, their actions have been subjected to increasing litigation and heightened constitutional scrutiny. Courts have been required to resolve the thorny constitutional attacks on state programs and procedures with limited precedential guidance. In this case, appellees have challenged Georgia's procedural and substantive balance of the individual, family, and social interests at stake in the voluntary commitment of a child to one of its regional mental hospitals.

The parties agree that our prior holdings have set out a general approach for testing challenged state procedures under a due process claim. Assuming the existence of a protectible property or liberty interest, the Court has required a balancing of a number of factors:

> First, the private interest that will be affected by the official action; second, the risk of an erroneous deprivation of such interest through the procedures used, and the probable value, if any, of additional or substitute procedural safeguards; and finally, the Government's interest, including the function involved and the fiscal and administrative burdens that the

additional or substitute procedural requirement would entail.
[*Mathews v. Eldridge* (1976), quoted in *Smith v. Organization of Foster Families* (1977).]

In applying these criteria, we must consider first the child's interest in not being committed. Normally, however, since this interest is inextricably linked with the parents' interest in and obligation for the welfare and health of the child, the private interest at stake is a combination of the child's and parents' concerns. Next, we must examine the State's interest in the procedures it has adopted for commitment and treatment of children. Finally, we must consider how well Georgia's procedures protect against arbitrariness in the decision to commit a child to a state mental hospital.

The Child's Interests

It is not disputed that a child, in common with adults, has a substantial liberty interest in not being confined unnecessarily for medical treatment, and that the state's involvement in the commitment decision constitutes state action under the Fourteenth Amendment. We also recognize that commitment sometimes produces adverse social consequences for the child because of the reaction of some to the discovery that the child has received psychiatric care.

This reaction, however, need not be equated with the community response resulting from being labeled by the state as delinquent, criminal, or mentally ill and possibly dangerous. The state, through its voluntary commitment procedures, does not "label" the child; it provides a diagnosis and treatment that medical specialists conclude the child requires. In terms of public reaction, the child who exhibits abnormal behavior may be seriously injured by an erroneous decision not to commit. Appellees overlook a significant source of the public reaction to the mentally ill, for what is truly "stigmatizing" is the symptomatology of a mental or emotional illness. The pattern of untreated, abnormal behavior—even if nondangerous—arouses at least as much negative reaction as treatment that becomes public knowledge. A person needing, but not receiving, appropriate medical care may well face even greater social ostracism resulting from the observable symptoms of an untreated disorder.

However, we need not decide what effect these factors might have in a different case. For purposes of this decision, we assume that a child has a protectible interest not only in being free of unnecessary bodily restraints but also in not being labeled erroneously by some persons because of an improper decision by the state hospital superintendent.

The Interests of Parents

We next deal with the interests of the parents who have decided, on the basis of their observations and independent professional recommendations, that their child needs institutional care. Appellees argue that the constitutional rights of the child are of such magnitude, and the likelihood of parental abuse is so great, that the parents' traditional interests in and responsibility for the upbringing of their child must be subordinated at least to the extent of providing a formal adversary hearing prior to a voluntary commitment.

Our jurisprudence historically has reflected Western civilization concepts of the family as a unit with broad parental authority over minor children. Our cases have consistently followed that course; our constitutional system long ago rejected any notion that a child is "the mere creature of the State" and, on the contrary, asserted that parents generally "have the right, coupled with the high duty, to recognize and prepare [their children] for additional obligations" [*Pierce v. Society of Sisters* (1925)]. Surely, this includes a "high duty" to recognize symptoms of illness and to seek and follow medical advice. The law's concept of the family rests on a presumption that parents possess what a child lacks in maturity, experience, and capacity for judgment required for making life's difficult decisions. More important, historically it

In Parham v. J.R. *(1979), the US Supreme Court ruled that a Georgia law allowing parents to commit their minor children to a mental hospital does not violate the minor's due process rights.* © BSIP/Universal Images Group/Getty Images.

has recognized that natural bonds of affection lead parents to act in the best interests of their children.

As with so many other legal presumptions, experience and reality may rebut what the law accepts as a starting point; the incidence of child neglect and abuse cases attests to this. That some parents "may at times be acting against the interests of their children," as was stated in *Bartley v. Kremens* (1977), creates a basis for caution, but is hardly a reason to discard wholesale those pages of human experience that teach that parents generally do act in the child's best interests. The statist notion that governmental power should supersede parental authority in all cases because some parents abuse and neglect children is repugnant to American tradition.

When Interests Collide

Nonetheless, we have recognized that a state is not without constitutional control over parental discretion in dealing with children when their physical or mental health is jeopardized. Moreover, the Court recently declared unconstitutional a state statute that granted parents an absolute veto over a minor child's decision to have an abortion. Appellees urge that these precedents limiting the traditional rights of parents, if viewed in the context of the liberty interest of the child and the likelihood of parental abuse, require us to hold that the parents' decision to have a child admitted to a mental hospital must be subjected to an exacting constitutional scrutiny, including a formal, adversary, pre-admission hearing.

Appellees' argument, however, sweeps too broadly. Simply because the decision of a parent is not agreeable to a child, or because it involves risks, does not automatically transfer the power to make that decision from the parents to some agency or officer of the state. The same characterizations can be made for a tonsillectomy, appendectomy, or other medical procedure. Most children, even in adolescence, simply are not able to make sound judgments concerning many decisions, including their need for medical care or treatment. Parents can and must make those judgments. Here, there is no finding by the District Court of even a single instance of bad faith by any parent of any member of appellees' class. We cannot assume that the result in *Meyer v. Nebraska* [1923] and *Pierce v. Society of Sisters* would have been different if the children there had announced a preference to learn only English or a preference to go to a public, rather than a church, school. The fact that a child may balk at hospitalization or complain about a parental refusal to provide cosmetic surgery does not diminish the parents' authority to decide what is best for the child. Neither state officials nor federal courts are equipped to review such parental decisions.

Appellees place particular reliance on *Planned Parenthood* [*of Central Missouri v. Danforth* (1976)], arguing that its holding indicates how little deference to parents is appropriate when the child is exercising a constitutional right. The basic situation in that case, however, was very different; *Planned Parenthood* involved an absolute parental veto over the child's ability to obtain an abortion. Parents in Georgia in no sense have an absolute right to commit their children to state mental hospitals; the statute requires the superintendent of each regional hospital to exercise independent judgment as to the child's need for confinement.

In defining the respective rights and prerogatives of the child and parent in the voluntary commitment setting, we conclude that our precedents permit the parents to retain a substantial, if not the dominant, role in the decision, absent a finding of neglect or abuse, and that the traditional presumption that the parents act in the best interests of their child should apply. We also conclude, however, that the child's rights and the nature of the commitment decision are such that parents cannot always have absolute and unreviewable discretion to decide whether to have a child institutionalized. They, of course, retain plenary authority to seek such care for their children, subject to a physician's independent examination and medical judgment.

SAMPLE STATE LAWS FOR INVOLUNTARY HOSPITALIZATION

Alabama	A minor under 18 years is a child and can be committed "voluntarily" without consent, but with parental consent (§ 12-15-90).
Alaska	A minor under 18 years is a child and can be committed "voluntarily" without consent, but with parental consent (Sec. 47.30.775).
Arizona	A minor under 18 years is a child and can be committed "voluntarily" without consent, but with parental consent (Arizona Revised Code §8-273).
Illinois	A minor 12 and older who objects must be discharged within 15 days, unless objection is withdrawn or a petition is filed for court review (405 ILCS 5/3-501).
Maryland	A minor under 18 years is a child and can be committed "voluntarily" without consent, but with parental consent which will not exceed 20 days (Maryland Code § 10-610).
Massachusetts	Minors 16 and 17 years old may be involuntary committed without consent, but with parental consent, not exceeding 90 days (M.G.L. c. 231, § 85P).
Minnesota	At age 16 and 17, if parent gives consent but child refuses, an independent examination is conducted to determine necessity to commit (Minnesota Statutes 253B.04).
Pennsylvania	A minor under 18 years is a child and can be committed "voluntarily" without consent, but with parental consent (50 Pennsylvania Code).
Utah	A minor under 18 years is a child and can be committed "voluntarily" without consent, but with parental consent (62A-15-705).
Virginia	A minor 14 years and older admitted without their consent, but the consent of their parent, shall be examined involuntarily (§ 16.1-339).
Washington	Under 18 is a child and can be committed without consent, needs parental consent, but may petition to be released (Revised Code of Washington 71.34).

Taken from: Vermont Legislature Research Service, "State Law Regarding Minor Consent to Psychiatric Commitment," 2007. www.uvm.edu/~vlrs.

The State's Role

The State obviously has a significant interest in confining the use of its costly mental health facilities to cases of genuine need. The Georgia program seeks first to determine whether the patient seeking admission has an illness that calls for inpatient treatment. To accomplish this purpose, the State has charged the superintendents of each regional hospital with the responsibility for determining, before authorizing an admission, whether a prospective patient is mentally ill and whether the patient will likely benefit from hospital care. In addition, the State has imposed a continuing duty on hospital superintendents to release any patient who has recovered to the point where hospitalization is no longer needed.

The State in performing its voluntarily assumed mission also has a significant interest in not imposing unnecessary procedural obstacles that may discourage the mentally ill or their families from seeking needed psychiatric assistance. The *parens patriae* [parent of the nation] interest in helping parents care for the mental health of their children cannot be fulfilled if the parents are unwilling to take advantage of the opportunities because the admission process is too onerous, too embarrassing, or too contentious. It is surely not idle to speculate as to how many parents who believe they are acting in good faith would forgo state-provided hospital care if such care is contingent on participation in an adversary proceeding designed to probe their motives and other private family matters in seeking the voluntary admission.

The State also has a genuine interest in allocating priority to the diagnosis and treatment of patients as soon as they are admitted to a hospital, rather than to time-consuming procedural minuets before the admission. One factor that must be considered is the utilization of the time of psychiatrists, psychologists, and other behavioral specialists in preparing for and participating in hearings, rather than performing the task for which their special training has fitted them. Behavioral experts in courtrooms and hearings are of little help to patients.

The *amici* brief of the American Psychiatric Association *et al.* points out at page 20 that the average staff psychiatrist in a hospital presently is able to devote only 47% of his time to direct patient care. One consequence of increasing the procedures the state must provide prior to a child's voluntary admission will be that mental health professionals will be diverted even more from the treatment of patients in order to travel to and participate in— and wait for—what could be hundreds—or even thousands—of hearings each year. Obviously the cost of these procedures would come from the public moneys the legislature intended for mental health care.

The Need for a Neutral Factfinder

We now turn to consideration of what process protects adequately the child's constitutional rights by reducing risks of error without unduly trenching on traditional parental authority and without undercutting "efforts to further the legitimate interests of both the state and the patient that are served by" voluntary commitments, [*Addington v. Texas* (1979)]. We conclude that the risk of error inherent in the parental decision to have a child institutionalized for mental health care is sufficiently great that some kind of inquiry should be made by a "neutral factfinder" to determine whether the statutory requirements for admission are satisfied. That inquiry must carefully probe the child's background using all available sources, including, but not limited to, parents, schools, and other social agencies. Of course, the review must also include an interview with the child. It is necessary that the decision-maker have the authority to refuse to admit any child who does not satisfy the medical standards for admission. Finally, it is necessary that the child's continuing need for commitment be reviewed periodically by a similarly independent procedure.

We are satisfied that such procedures will protect the child from an erroneous admission decision in a way that neither unduly burdens the states nor inhibits parental decisions to seek state help.

Due process has never been thought to require that the neutral and detached trier of fact be law trained or a judicial or administrative officer. Surely, this is the case as to medical decisions, for "neither judges nor administrative hearing officers are better qualified than psychiatrists to render psychiatric judgments" [*In re Roger S.* (1977) (Clark, J., dissenting)]. Thus, a staff physician will suffice, so long as he or she is free to evaluate independently the child's mental and emotional condition and need for treatment.

It is not necessary that the deciding physician conduct a formal or quasi-formal hearing. A state is free to require such a hearing, but due process is not violated by use of informal, traditional medical investigative techniques. Since well established medical procedures already exist, we do not undertake to outline with specificity precisely what this investigation must involve. The mode and procedure of medical diagnostic procedures is not the business of judges. What is best for a child is an individual medical decision that must be left to the judgment of physicians in each case. We do no more than emphasize that the decision should represent an independent judgment of what the child requires and that all sources of information that are traditionally relied on by physicians and behavioral specialists should be consulted.

> "We find that a mature minor may
> exercise a common law right to consent
> to or refuse medical care."

Mature Minors Have the Right to Consent to or Refuse Medical Care

The Illinois Supreme Court's Decision

Howard C. Ryan

In the following viewpoint, Justice Howard C. Ryan, writing for the majority on the Supreme Court of Illinois, argues that both constitutional law and common law support the rights of minors to make decisions about their health care in certain situations. Ryan claims that maturity is a relevant factor in determining the ability to consent to medical treatment. He claims that the US Supreme Court has granted minors certain constitutional rights that support medical choices in certain contexts. He also claims that several state courts have identified the rights of minors to make medical decisions. Ryan concludes that although minors have a right to consent to or refuse medical care, this must be balanced against state interests and family interests. Ryan was a justice of the Supreme Court of Illinois from 1970 to 1990, serving as its chief justice from 1982 to 1985.

Howard C. Ryan, Majority opinion, *In re E.G.*, Supreme Court of Illinois, November 13, 1989.

Appellee, E.G., a 17-year-old woman, contracted leukemia and needed blood transfusions in the treatment of the disease. E.G. and her mother, Rosie Denton, refused to consent to the transfusions, contending that acceptance of blood would violate personal religious convictions rooted in their membership in the Jehovah's Witness faith. Appellant, the State of Illinois, filed a neglect petition in juvenile court in the circuit court of Cook County. The trial court entered an order finding E.G. to be neglected, and appointed a guardian to consent to the transfusions on E.G.'s behalf.

The appellate court reversed the trial court in part. The court held that E.G. was a "mature minor," and therefore could refuse the blood transfusions through the exercise of her first amendment right to freely exercise her religion. Nevertheless, the court affirmed the finding of neglect against Denton....

A Refusal of Medical Treatment

In February of 1987, E.G. was diagnosed as having acute non-lymphatic leukemia, a malignant disease of the white blood cells. When E.G. and her mother, Rosie Denton, were informed that treatment of the disease would involve blood transfusions, they refused to consent to this medical procedure on the basis of their religious beliefs. As Jehovah's Witnesses, both E.G. and her mother desired to observe their religion's prohibition against the "eating" of blood. Mrs. Denton did authorize any other treatment and signed a waiver absolving the medical providers of liability for failure to administer transfusions.

As a result of Denton's and E.G.'s refusal to assent to blood transfusions, the State filed a neglect petition in juvenile court. At the initial hearing on February 25, 1987, Dr. Stanley Yachnin testified that E.G. had approximately one-fifth to one-sixth the normal oxygen-carrying capacity of her blood and consequently was excessively fatigued and incoherent. He stated that without blood transfusions, E.G. would likely die within a month. Dr. Yachnin testified that the transfusions, along with chemotherapy,

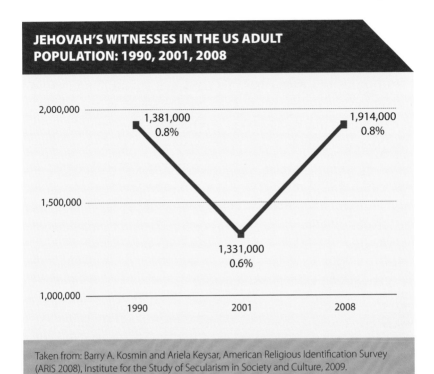

JEHOVAH'S WITNESSES IN THE US ADULT POPULATION: 1990, 2001, 2008

- 1990: 1,381,000 (0.8%)
- 2001: 1,331,000 (0.6%)
- 2008: 1,914,000 (0.8%)

Taken from: Barry A. Kosmin and Ariela Keysar, American Religious Identification Survey (ARIS 2008), Institute for the Study of Secularism in Society and Culture, 2009.

achieve remission of the disease in about 80% of all patients so afflicted. Continued treatment, according to Dr. Yachnin, would involve the utilization of drugs and more transfusions. The long-term prognosis is not optimistic, as the survival rate for patients such as E.G. is 20 to 25%.

Dr. Yachnin stated that he discussed the proposed course of treatment with E.G. He testified that E.G. was competent to understand the consequences of accepting or rejecting treatment, and he was impressed with her maturity and the sincerity of her beliefs. Dr. Yachnin's observations regarding E.G.'s competency were corroborated by the testimony of Jane McAtee, the associate general counsel for the University of Chicago Hospital. At the conclusion of this hearing, the trial Judge entered an order appointing McAtee temporary guardian, and authorizing her to consent to transfusions on E.G.'s behalf.

On April 8, 1987, further hearings were held on this matter. E.G., having received several blood transfusions, was strong enough to take the stand. She testified that the decision to refuse blood transfusions was her own and that she fully understood the nature of her disease and the consequences of her decision. She indicated that her decision was not based on any wish to die, but instead was grounded in her religious convictions. E.G. further stated that when informed that she would undergo transfusions, she asked to be sedated prior to the administration of the blood. She testified that the court's decision upset her, and said: "It seems as if everything that I wanted or believe in was just being disregarded."

The Importance of Maturity

Several other witnesses gave their opinions extolling E.G.'s maturity and the sincerity of her religious beliefs. One witness was Dr. Littner, a psychiatrist who has special expertise in evaluating the maturity and competency of minors. Based on interviews with E.G. and her family, Dr. Littner expressed his opinion that E.G. had the maturity level of an 18 to 21 year old. He further concluded that E.G. had the competency to make an informed decision to refuse the blood transfusions, even if this choice was fatal.

On May 18, 1987, the trial court ruled that E.G. was medically neglected, and appointed a guardian to consent to medical treatment. The court felt this was in E.G.'s best interests. The court did state, however, that E.G. was "a mature 17-year-old individual," that E.G. reached her decision on an independent basis, and that she was "fully aware that death [was] assured absent treatment." The court noted that it considered E.G.'s maturity and the religion of her and her parents, and that it gave great weight to the wishes of E.G. Nevertheless, the court felt that the State's interest in this case was greater than the interest E.G. and her mother had in refusing to consent to treatment. The court concluded its ruling by encouraging E.G. to appeal.

On appeal, the order of the trial court pertaining to E.G.'s right to refuse treatment was vacated in part and modified in part. The appellate court observed that this court, in *In re Estate of Brooks* (1965), held that an adult Jehovah's Witness had a first amendment right to refuse blood transfusions. The appellate court then extended the holding in *Brooks* to include "mature minors," deriving this extension from cases in which the United States Supreme Court allowed "mature minors" to consent to abortions without parental approval through the exercise of constitutional privacy rights. Although the United States Supreme Court has not broadened this constitutional right of minors beyond abortion cases, the appellate court found such an extension "inevitable." Relying on our Emancipation of Mature Minors Act, the court held that a mature minor may exercise a constitutional right to refuse medical treatment.

The appellate court noted that E.G., at the time of trial, was only six months shy of her eighteenth birthday, and that the trial court believed E.G. to be a mature individual. Based on these facts, the appellate court declared that E.G. was partially emancipated and therefore had the right to refuse transfusions. The court, however, affirmed the finding of neglect against Denton, E.G.'s mother. . . .

The Ability to Consent to Medical Treatment

The paramount issue raised by this appeal is whether a minor like E.G. has a right to refuse medical treatment. In Illinois, an adult has a common law right to refuse medical treatment, even if it is of a life-sustaining nature. This court has also held that an adult may refuse life-saving blood transfusions on first amendment free exercise of religion grounds. An infant child, however, can be compelled to accept life-saving medical treatment over the objections of her parents. In the matter before us, E.G. was a minor, but one who was just months shy of her eighteenth birthday, and an individual that the record indicates was mature for

In 1989 the Supreme Court of Illinois ruled that minors have the right to consent to or refuse medical care in certain situations. © Camille Tokerud/Iconica/Getty Images.

her age. Although the age of majority in Illinois is 18, that age is not an impenetrable barrier that magically precludes a minor from possessing and exercising certain rights normally associated with adulthood. Numerous exceptions are found in this jurisdiction and others which treat minors as adults under specific circumstances.

In Illinois, our legislature enacted "An Act in relation to the performance of medical, dental or surgical procedures on and counseling for minors" (the Consent by Minors to Medical Operations Act), which grants minors the legal capacity to consent to medical treatment in certain situations. For example, a minor 12 years or older may seek medical attention on her own if she believes she has venereal disease or is an alcoholic or drug addict. Similarly, an individual under 18 who is married or pregnant may validly consent to treatment. Thus, if E.G. would have been married she could have consented to or, presumably, refused treatment. Also, a minor 16 or older may be declared emancipated under the Emancipation of Mature Minors Act, and thereby control his or her own health care decisions. These two acts, when read together in a complementary fashion, indicate that the legislature did not intend that there be an absolute 18-year-old age barrier prohibiting minors from consenting to medical treatment. . . .

Constitutional and Common Law

Another area of the law where minors are treated as adults is constitutional law, including the constitutional right of abortion. The United States Supreme Court has adopted a mature minor doctrine, which allows women under the age of majority to undergo abortions without parental consent. In the abortion rights context, the Court has noted: "Constitutional rights do not mature and come into being magically only when one attains the state-defined age of majority. Minors, as well as adults, are protected by the Constitution and possess constitutional rights." [*Planned Parenthood of Central Missouri v. Danforth* (1976)]. Moreover, children enjoy the protection of other constitutional rights, including the right of privacy, freedom of expression, freedom from unreasonable searches and seizures, and procedural due process. Nevertheless, the Supreme Court has not held that a constitutionally based right to refuse medical treatment exists, either for adults or minors. While we find the language from the cases cited above instructive, we do not feel, as the appellate court did, that an extension of the constitutional mature minor doctrine to the case at bar is "inevitable." These cases do show, however, that no "bright line" age restriction of 18 is tenable in restricting the rights of mature minors, whether the rights be based on constitutional or other grounds. Accordingly, we hold that in addition to these constitutionally based rights expressly delineated by the Supreme Court, mature minors may possess and exercise rights regarding medical care that are rooted in this State's common law.

The common law right to control one's health care was also the basis for the right of an incompetent patient to refuse life-sustaining treatment through a surrogate in *In re Estate of Longeway* [1989]. While the issue before us in this case is not exactly the same as in *Longeway*, the foundation of the common law right here and in *Longeway* is the same. We see no reason why this right of dominion over one's own person should not extend to mature minors. Furthermore, we find support for this conclusion in a decision of one of our sister States. In *Cardwell v. Bechtol* (Tenn. 1987), the Tennessee Supreme Court held that a mature minor had the capacity to consent to medical procedures based on the common law of that State. The court noted that the mature minor doctrine is not a recent development in the law: "recognition that minors achieve varying degrees of maturity and responsibility (capacity) has been part of the common law for well over a century."

In *Cardwell*, the Tennessee court held that a minor 17 years, 7 months old was mature enough to consent to medical treatment. We note that in other jurisdictions, courts have ordered health care for minors over the objections of the minors' parents. These cases, however, involve minors who were younger than E.G. or the minor in *Cardwell*. Moreover, the issue in the above cases was not whether a minor could assert a right to control medical treatment decisions, but whether the minor's parents could refuse treatment on behalf of their child. Here, E.G. contends she was mature enough to have controlled her own health care. We find that she may have done so if indeed she would have been adjudged mature.

Two Principles for Judicial Consideration

The trial Judge must determine whether a minor is mature enough to make health care choices on her own. An exception to this, of course, is if the legislature has provided otherwise, as in the Consent by Minors to Medical Operations Act. We feel the intervention of a Judge is appropriate for two reasons.

First, Illinois public policy values the sanctity of life. When a minor's health and life are at stake, this policy becomes a critical consideration. A minor may have a long and fruitful life ahead that an immature, foolish decision could jeopardize. Consequently, when the trial Judge weighs the evidence in making a determination of whether a minor is mature enough to handle a health care decision, he must find proof of this maturity by clear and convincing evidence.

Second, the State has a *parens patriae* [parent of the nation] power to protect those incompetent to protect themselves. "It is well-settled that the State as *parens patriae* has a special duty to protect minors and, if necessary, make vital decisions as to whether to submit a minor to necessary treatment where the condition is life threatening, as wrenching and distasteful as such actions may be." [*In re Hamilton* (Tenn. App. 1983)]. The State's *parens patriae* power pertaining to minors is strongest when the minor is immature and thus incompetent (lacking in capacity) to make these decisions on her own. The *parens patriae* authority fades, however, as the minor gets older and disappears upon her reaching adulthood. The State interest in protecting a mature minor in these situations will vary depending upon the nature of the medical treatment involved. Where the health care issues are potentially life threatening, the State's *parens patriae* interest is greater than if the health care matter is less consequential.

Therefore, the trial Judge must weigh these two principles against the evidence he receives of a minor's maturity. If the evidence is clear and convincing that the minor is mature enough to appreciate the consequences of her actions, and that the minor is mature enough to exercise the judgment of an adult, then the mature minor doctrine affords her the common law right to consent to or refuse medical treatment. As we stated in *Longeway*, however, this common law right is not absolute. The right must be balanced against four State interests: (1) the preservation of life; (2) protecting the interests of third parties; (3) prevention of suicide; and (4) maintaining the ethical integrity of the medical profession. Of these four concerns, protecting the interests of third parties is clearly the most significant here. The principal third parties in these cases would be parents, guardians, adult siblings, and other relatives. If a parent or guardian opposes an unemancipated mature minor's refusal to consent to treatment for a life-threatening health problem, this opposition would weigh heavily against the minor's right to refuse. In this case, for example, had E.G. refused the transfusions against the wishes of her mother, then the court would have given serious consideration to her mother's desires.

Nevertheless, in this case both E.G. and her mother agreed that E.G. should turn down the blood transfusions. They based this refusal primarily on religious grounds, contending that the first amendment free exercise clause entitles a mature minor to decline medical care when it contravenes sincerely held religious beliefs. Because we find that a mature minor may exercise a common law right to consent to or refuse medical care, we decline to address the constitutional issue.

> "When a parent fails to provide medical care to his or her child . . . and causes the death of the child . . . the parent is guilty of second-degree reckless homicide."

Religious Freedom Does Not Permit Parents to Deny Children Life-Saving Treatment

The Wisconsin Supreme Court's Decision

Shirley S. Abrahamson

In the following viewpoint, Shirley S. Abrahamson, writing for the majority on the Wisconsin Supreme Court, argues that a Wisconsin statute that allows parents to engage in prayer healing without automatically being guilty of child abuse does not protect them from the criminal charge of homicide in failing to seek life-saving medical treatment. Abrahamson claims that the parents in the case at hand, whose eleven-year-old daughter died from treatable diabetes, are not protected by the treatment-through-prayer provision in the law and should have known that the law would not protect them from such a failure to medically treat their daughter. Abrahamson has been chief justice of the Wisconsin Supreme Court since 1996, having served as a justice of that court since 1976.

Shirley S. Abrahamson, Majority opinion, *State v. Neumann*, Wisconsin Supreme Court, July 3, 2013.

Eleven-year-old Madeline Kara Neumann died tragically on Easter Sunday, March 23, 2008, from diabetic ketoacidosis resulting from untreated juvenile onset diabetes mellitus. Kara died when her father and mother, Dale R. Neumann and Leilani E. Neumann, chose to treat Kara's undiagnosed serious illness with prayer, rather than medicine. Each parent was charged with and convicted of the second-degree reckless homicide of Madeline Kara Neumann in violation of Wis. Stat. § 940.06(1) (2009-10), in separate trials with different juries. . . .

A Child's Death

According to the undisputed testimony, the facts relating to the child's health and the parents' conduct were essentially the same in each jury trial and are set forth here.

Madeline Kara Neumann died at 3:30 p.m. on Sunday, March 23, 2008, from diabetic ketoacidosis resulting from untreated juvenile onset diabetes mellitus. Kara had suffered gradually worsening symptoms for a few weeks before her death, leading to frequent thirst and urination, dehydration, weakness, and exhaustion, yet to the casual observer, as the State and parents stipulated, Kara would have appeared healthy as late as the Thursday before she died.

On the Friday night before she died, Kara was too tired to finish her homework and ate her dinner in her bedroom. On Saturday, the day before her death, Kara slept all day after asking to stay home from work at the family's coffee shop. When her mother returned home from work Saturday afternoon, Kara was pale and her legs were skinny and blue. Her mother knew that something was wrong and called her husband into the room. The parents began rubbing Kara's legs and praying for her.

A Belief in Spiritual Healing

The Neumanns do not belong to any identifiable church or religious organization, but identify as Pentecostals. They believe that there are spiritual root causes to sickness and that their prayer and strong religious beliefs will cure any health problems they encounter.

Kara's parents had not always relied only on spiritual healing in the past. All of their children were born in a hospital and vaccinated. The father went to a chiropractor for some ten years for back pain but believed that he was relieved of his pain through prayer. The parents decided not to go to doctors for treatment anymore, out of a belief that they would be "putting the doctor before God," amounting to idolatry and sin.

The father testified that he believed that his family's overall health had improved since the family had stopped going to doctors, and thus, when the parents realized that Kara was ill on Saturday afternoon, they began to pray.

Soon after the parents began to pray, they enlisted the help of others, calling family and friends asking them to pray for Kara as well. The father sent a mass e-mail at 4:58 p.m. on Saturday to a listserv of like-minded people, which read:

> Subject: Help our daughter needs emergency prayer!!!
>
> We need agreement in prayer over our youngest daughter, who is very weak and pale at the moment with hardly any strength.

The parents testified that they did not know specifically what was wrong with Kara, thinking it could be a fever or the flu, but they knew it was serious and needed attention, so they prayed. When informed of Kara's condition, Kara's maternal grandmother suggested they take her to a doctor. The mother replied, "No, she'll be fine, God will heal her."

A Worsening Illness

When the family took a break from prayer to eat dinner Saturday evening, Kara remained in bed. While the family ate, Kara went to use the bathroom. She fell off the toilet. Her father picked her up and carried her to the couch in the living room where they could watch her. The family stayed up late praying over Kara, until finally, the parents went to sleep because they "were exhausted . . . [from the] non-stop praying and just continually trusting in the Lord."

According to trial testimony, by the time the family went to sleep Saturday night, Kara was unable to walk or talk. Kara's brother Luke testified that he believed Kara was in a coma. Kara's siblings stayed with her throughout the night while she lay limp and unresponsive on the couch.

When her father awoke early Sunday morning, around 5:00 a.m., Kara was still pale, limp, unconscious, and unresponsive, although she sometimes moaned in response to friends and family members calling her name. Her breathing was less labored than it had been the previous night.

Kara's mother continued to call friends and relatives to tell them about Kara's condition and ask for prayers. Various people came by the home on Sunday to pray and later, in trial testimony, witnesses characterized Kara's condition as a coma. Still, family and friends testified that everyone was at complete peace and did not sense any danger in Kara's condition.

Kara's father testified that death was never on their minds. He testified that he knew Kara was sick but was "never to the alarm of death," and even after she died, her father thought that Jesus would bring Kara back from the dead, as he did with Lazarus.

Concern from Family and Friends

The parents and friends testified that the parents took tangible steps to help Kara. The mother tried to feed Kara soup and water with a syringe, but the liquid just dribbled out of Kara's mouth. The father tried to sit Kara up, but she was unable to hold herself up. At some point, Kara involuntarily urinated on herself while lying unresponsive on the couch, so they carried her upstairs and gave her a quick sponge bath while she lay on the bathroom floor.

At one point, Kara's maternal grandfather suggested by telephone that they give Kara Pedialyte, a nutritional supplement, in order to maintain the nutrients in her body. The mother re-

Parental Rights and Religious Rights

It is cardinal with us that the custody, care and nurture of the child reside first in the parents, whose primary function and freedom include preparation for obligations the state can neither supply nor hinder. And it is in recognition of this that these decisions have respected the private realm of family life which the state cannot enter.

But the family itself is not beyond regulation in the public interest, as against a claim of religious liberty. And neither rights of religion nor rights of parenthood are beyond limitation. Acting to guard the general interest in the youth's well-being, the state as *parens patriae* [parent of the nation] may restrict the parent's control by requiring school attendance, regulating or prohibiting the child's labor, and in many other ways. Its authority is not nullified merely because the parent grounds his claim to control the child's course of conduct on religion or conscience. Thus, he cannot claim freedom from compulsory vaccination for the child more than for himself on religious grounds. The right to practice religion freely does not include liberty to expose the community or the child to communicable disease or the latter to ill health or death.

Wiley Blount Rutledge, Majority opinion,
Prince v. Commonwealth of Massachusetts,
US Supreme Court, January 31, 1944.

sponded that giving Kara Pedialyte would be taking away the glory from God. Kara's mother had told another visiting friend that she believed that Kara was under "spiritual attack."

Friends Althea and Randall Wormgoor testified that they arrived at the Neumanns' home on Sunday at approximately 1:30 p.m. The Wormgoors saw that Kara was extremely ill and nonresponsive. Her eyes were partially open but they believed she needed immediate medical attention. Randall Wormgoor pulled Kara's father aside and told him that if it was his daughter, he would take her to the hospital. The father responded that the idea had crossed his mind, and he had suggested it to his wife, but she believed Kara's illness was a test of faith for their family and that the Lord would heal Kara.

During this conversation, Althea Wormgoor noticed a distinct twitch from Kara's mouth, which startled her. Thinking that Kara had stopped breathing, Randall Wormgoor called 911. Unbeknownst to those in the home, police and emergency medical personnel were already en route to the Neumann home, having received a call from Ariel Neff, the mother's sister-in-law in California, explaining that Kara might be in a coma and that her parents refused to take her to a doctor. Ariel Neff's call was recorded at 2:33 p.m. on Sunday.

A Treatable Condition

Police and emergency medical personnel arrived to find the parents praying over their extremely skinny, pulseless daughter. The paramedics transported Kara to the hospital, where attempts to revive her were unsuccessful. In the ambulance, the paramedics noticed a fruity odor, a known symptom of untreated diabetes. They took a blood sample to measure her blood sugar but her blood sugar level was too high for the monitor to read. Reports from emergency medical personnel and doctors indicated that Kara appeared extremely skinny and malnourished, with a bluish-gray skin color, and was dehydrated and skeleton-like, with a pronounced pelvic bone, eye sockets, cheekbones, and ribs.

According to the emergency room doctor's testimony, Kara was "cachectic," which is a term normally used to describe a cancer patient—very malnourished, thin, and smaller than you expect of the age. The emergency room doctor diagnosed Kara's cause of death as diabetic ketoacidosis, which was later confirmed by the medical examiner's autopsy.

The emergency room doctor also testified that if a child is brought into the emergency room suffering from diabetic ketoacidosis but is still breathing and still has a heartbeat, the prognosis for survival is very good. A pediatric endocrinologist testified that, if treated, diabetic ketoacidosis has a 99.8% survival rate. He testified that Kara's disease was treatable and her chances of survival were high until "well into the day of her death."

Each parent was charged with, and convicted of, second-degree reckless homicide in connection with Kara's death. Each was sentenced to 180 days in jail and ten years of probation. Each was sentenced to serve 30 days in jail each year for six years, alternating the months of March and September with the other parent. The circuit court granted a motion to stay the jail sentence pending this appeal.

The Wisconsin Statutes

The parents argue that their convictions for choosing treatment through prayer violate due process fair notice requirements. . . .

In considering whether the criminal statutes at issue satisfy the requirements of due process fair notice, we begin by setting forth the texts of the statutes involved.

The parents were convicted of violating Wis. Stat. § 940.06(1), the second-degree reckless homicide statute. . . .

In order to compare the four statutes more easily, we insert the defined terms into the text of each statute and reprint the four statutes below:

> Wis. Stat. § 940.06(1) Whoever creates an unreasonable and substantial risk of death or bodily injury which creates a substantial risk of death, or other enumerated physical injuries, to another human being and is aware of that risk and causes the death of another human being is guilty of a Class D Felony.

> Wis. Stat. § 948.03(3)(a) Whoever creates a situation of unreasonable risk of harm to and demonstrates a conscious disregard for the safety of the child and causes bodily injury which creates a substantial risk of death, or other enumerated physical injuries, to a child is guilty of a Class E Felony.

Wis. Stat. § 948.03(3)(c) Whoever creates a situation of un-reasonable risk of harm to and demonstrates a conscious dis-regard for the safety of a child and causes bodily harm to a child by conduct which creates a high probability of bodily injury which creates a substantial risk of death, or other enu-merated physical injuries, is guilty of a Class H Felony.

Wis. Stat. § 948.03(6) Treatment through prayer. A per-son is not guilty of an offense under this section [§ 948.03] solely because he or she provides a child with treatment by spiritual means through prayer alone for healing in accor-dance with the religious method of healing permitted under s. 48.981(3) (c)4. or 448.03(6) in lieu of medical or surgical treatment. . . .

The Treatment-Through-Prayer Provision

On its face, the treatment-through-prayer provision does not immunize a parent from any criminal liability other than that created by the criminal child abuse statute. There is no cross-reference between the criminal child abuse statute and the second-degree reckless homicide statute. No one reading the treatment-through-prayer provision should expect protection from criminal liability under any other statute. . . .

Provisions regarding treatment through prayer appear in several instances in the Wisconsin statutes. Taken together, these statutes evidence the legislature's balancing in each instance of the interests of persons who rely on treatment through prayer and the State's interest in protecting individuals. The statutes demonstrate that the legislature has carefully considered under what circumstances it is willing to allow reliance on treatment through prayer for those who believe in the efficacy of such treat-ment and when it is not. If the legislature intended a treatment-through-prayer provision to apply across the board to all crimi-nal statutes, the legislature could have used different language or placed a treatment-through-prayer provision in Chapter 939 with other defenses to criminal liability.

Thus, the text of the treatment-through-prayer provision, Wis. Stat. § 948.03(6), does not and cannot lead parents to expect that they are immune from criminal prosecution for second-degree reckless homicide.

The Fair Notice Claim

Rather than rely on the statutory treatment-through-prayer provision as explicitly protecting them from prosecution under the second-degree reckless homicide statute, the parents assert that the interplay of Wis. Stat. § 940.06(1), the second-degree reckless homicide statute, and § 948.03, the criminal child abuse statute (including the treatment-through-prayer provision), creates a lack of "fair notice" of prohibited conduct.

The parents' fair notice argument turns on the phrase "great bodily harm," which appears in the three statutory provisions at issue: Wis. Stat. §§ 940.06(1), 948.03 (3) (a), and 948.03(3) (c). "Great bodily harm" means bodily injury that creates a substantial risk of death or other enumerated physical injuries. Wis. Stat. § 939.22(14).

The parents contend that there is no legal difference between the conduct governed by the three statutes: "This 'substantial risk of death' that creates criminal liability under reckless homicide is the same 'substantial risk of death' explicitly protected in the prayer treatment exception." Even if there is a line between the statutes in theory, the parents aver that the line is too difficult to define or conceptualize.

The Parents' Argument

Accordingly, the parents maintain that a prayer-treating parent is protected up to and including the point at which the child experiences great bodily injury that means, among other things, a substantial risk of death. The parents read Wis. Stat. § 948.03(6) as telling prayer-healing parents that until a child's medical

Dale and Leilani Neumann leave the Marathon County Courthouse in Wausau, Wisconsin, in 2009. The Wisconsin Supreme Court found Leilani guilty of second-degree reckless homicide for failing to seek life-saving medical treatment for her daughter. © Corey Schjoth/Wausau Daily Herald/Associated Press.

condition progresses "to at least some point beyond a 'substantial risk of death,' they are immune from prosecution."

The parents interpret "the point beyond a 'substantial risk of death'" in the present cases as being the exact moment that

Kara died. The parents assert that up until Kara stopped breathing, their choice of treatment through prayer was a statutorily protected response to the "substantial risk of death" that Kara was experiencing. They assert that "[a]s 911 was called as soon as Kara stopped breathing," the "line" protecting prayer-treating parents "was never crossed."

The parents assert there is no boundary, no clear moment when they were on notice that their failure to provide medical care had crossed the line between the protection offered under Wis. Stat. § 948.03(6) and liability under Wis. Stat. § 940.06(1). The parents argue that the only dividing line between legality and illegality of the parents' conduct is the happenstance of death, and that this dividing line is too vague and unclear to provide sufficient notice in the present case.

Using this reasoning, the parents conclude that due process fair notice has been violated because they were convicted for conduct that the State told them was protected. They allege that the conflicting legal provisions violate due process by failing to furnish fair notice of what conduct is illegal.

Both the State and parents cite case law from other states that have addressed a due process fair notice challenge to support their respective positions. Most cases lend support to the State's position. A minority of cases lends support to the parents' position. The parents distinguish the cases favoring the State's position, and the State distinguishes the cases favoring the parents' position, each noting the differences in the statutes of other states and in the facts of the cases. The laws and facts are different in these non-Wisconsin cases, but the discussions and applications of the due process fair notice requirements by other state courts have been helpful in our analysis. . . .

A Homicidal Failure to Provide Care

We conclude that the second-degree reckless homicide statute and the criminal child abuse statute are sufficiently distinct that a parent has fair notice of conduct that is protected and conduct that is unprotected. The statutes are definite enough to provide a standard of conduct for those whose activities are proscribed and those whose conduct is protected. A reader of the treatment-through-prayer provision cannot reasonably conclude that he or she can, with impunity, use prayer treatment as protection against all criminal charges. The four statutes are not unconstitutional on due process fair notice grounds.

In sum, when a parent fails to provide medical care to his or her child, creates an unreasonable and substantial risk of death or great bodily harm, is aware of that risk, and causes the death of the child, the parent is guilty of second-degree reckless homicide.

This crime is substantially different from the crimes punished under the criminal child abuse statute. When a parent fails to provide medical care when there is a duty to act, creates a situation of unreasonable risk of harm to and demonstrates a conscious disregard for the safety of the child, and causes great bodily harm, the parent is guilty of violating Wis. Stat. § 948.03 (3) (a).

When a parent fails to provide medical care when there is a duty to act, creates a situation of unreasonable risk of harm to and demonstrates a conscious disregard for the safety of the child, and causes bodily harm to a child by conduct that creates a high probability of great bodily harm, the parent is guilty of violating Wis. Stat. § 948.03(3) (c).

A parent is not guilty of violating Wis. Stat. § 948.03(3) (a) and (3) (c) "solely because he or she provides a child with treatment by spiritual means through prayer alone for healing in accordance with the religious method of healing permitted under s. 48. 981 (3) (c)4. or 448.03(6) in lieu of medical or surgical treatment." Wis. Stat. § 948.03(6).

The juries could reasonably find that by failing to call for medical assistance when Kara was seriously ill and in a coma-like condition for 12 to 14 hours, the parents were creating an unreasonable and substantial risk of Kara's death, were subjectively aware of that risk, and caused her death. On the record before it, each jury could reasonably find that the State proved the elements of second-degree reckless homicide under Wis. Stat. § 940.06(1).

> *"Parents should be accorded the same immunity from prosecution when their cures fail as doctors are in the same circumstances."*

Religious Freedom Protects Parents' Health Care Decisions for Children

A.M. Rogers

In the following viewpoint, A. M. Rogers argues that the propensity of state courts to order medical treatment for children over their parents' wishes is threatening freedom. She gives several examples where parents have been taken to court either to mandate treatment for their children or criminally prosecute them for the failure to medically treat their children. Rogers claims that not allowing parents to make their own decisions about the medical treatment of their children involves a double standard that privileges science over all other possible cures, such as prayer. Rogers is an attorney and physicist in Ormond Beach, Florida.

The constitutional guarantee of religious freedom has often butted heads with the state. Though religious freedom was once the cornerstone of this country, its position has been slowly

A.M. Rogers, "Saving Sick Children from State Science," *The Freeman*, vol. 43, no. 6, June 1993, pp. 214–218. Copyright © 1993 by The Foundation for Economic Education. All rights reserved. Reproduced by permission.

eroded. And the state has justified this erosion by deference to what the law has turned into another god—science. The area of children's health and well-being has become one of the major battlegrounds of religious freedom.

Medical Treatment and the State

As early as 1880, a state removed children from a parent's care because the parent had not sought treatment from a medical doctor. In the case of *In Heinemann's Appeal* [1880], a Pennsylvania court found the father guilty of neglect of a child under the state statute because he had himself treated his wife and three other children who were sick with diphtheria. At the time, diphtheria was sweeping through parts of Europe and the United States. And interestingly, the first effective diphtheria antitoxin was not developed until 1890, by a German bacteriologist. Other Pennsylvania cases in the early 1900s held parents guilty of manslaughter for the failure to provide their children with medical treatment despite religious objections.

In almost every state today, whether the parents fail to seek medical treatment for a child based on the parents' own secular perceptions of the best interest of the child or their most fervent religious beliefs, the state can intrude and the parents can be prosecuted criminally.

According to the *American Law Reports*: "It has been settled that a state, as *parens patriae* [parent of the nation], may order medical treatment to save the life of a child notwithstanding the parents' religious objections to the treatment."

In 1967 in Washington, a group of Jehovah's Witnesses brought suit in opposition to a state statute that allowed the courts to order medical treatment, including blood transfusions, for children without parental consent. Jehovah's Witnesses believe that the act of receiving blood or blood products precludes a person from resurrection and everlasting life after death. In the case of *Jehovah's Witnesses in the State of Washington et. al. v. Kings County Hospital Unit No. 1*, the plaintiffs argued against the statute on a variety of grounds. Among others, they argued that it denied their right to family privacy afforded them by the U.S. Constitution's Ninth and Fourteenth amendments; that it denied them equal protection under the law since the state protects the religious liberty and parental rights of all other citizens and all other religions; that since the plaintiffs have a deep sense of responsibility as a family, they have the right to decide what medical treatment they will accept for their children; and, that the plaintiffs have been denied life, liberty, and property without due process of the law as guaranteed them by the Constitution's Fifth Amendment and made applicable to the state by the Fourteenth Amendment.

The state's highest court did not find any of these grounds persuasive. The court concluded that religious freedom does not include the freedom to expose children to ill health or death and that the state has the right to intervene in the name of health and welfare in these circumstances.

Treatment Ordered by State Courts

The U.S. Supreme Court typically has refused to hear similar cases. The high courts in New Jersey and Illinois also overruled parents who are Jehovah's Witnesses when they objected to their children having a court-ordered blood transfusion and both these cases were refused review by the Supreme Court.

In a 1991 case in Massachusetts, a hospital sought authority to permit and administer a blood transfusion to an 8-year-old girl over her parents' religious objections.

The McCauley parents had taken their daughter Elisha to the hospital for medical tests. The tests made an initial determination of leukemia, but the doctors wanted to do a bone marrow aspiration to determine with greater certainty whether Elisha did have leukemia. However, the doctors felt this procedure could not be performed safely unless they first increased Elisha's critically low hematocrit reading by giving her a blood transfusion.

Jehovah's Witnesses attend a convention in Oklahoma City in 2012. They believe receiving a blood transfusion goes against their religion; this belief has been the subject of numerous court cases involving religious freedom. © Mike Andrews/The Lawton Constitution/Associated Press.

The Massachusetts State Supreme Court here found three interests at stake: the natural rights of the parents, the child's interests, and the state's interests. The court then concluded that the interests of the child and the interests of the state outweighed the parents' rights to refuse medical treatment.

In these cases, the Jehovah's Witnesses were not opposed to medical treatment but only the blood transfusions. Similarly, in a 1972 Pennsylvania case, the mother, a Jehovah's Witness, agreed to the surgery but refused to consent to the blood transfusion. No doctor would perform the surgery, however, without prior consent to a blood transfusion, should it become necessary. A hospital director initiated these court proceedings under a state statute authorizing court-ordered treatment for children being deprived of the proper or necessary medical or surgical care. The child here had survived polio but was now no longer able to walk because of both obesity and curvature of the spine. The lower court authorized surgery on the spine and the concomitant blood transfusion. But the higher court reversed this order noting that the boy's condition was not life threatening.

The Criminal Prosecution of Parents

In other cases, the question of court-ordered medical treatments turns into cases of criminal prosecution.

In a 1985 Pennsylvania case [*com. v. Barnhart*], a couple was found guilty of involuntary manslaughter and endangering the welfare of a child in the death of their 2 1/2-year-old son. The parents had not sought any medical treatment outside their own religious treatment of their son, who eventually died of a cancerous tumor.

In Indiana, a jury found a mother and father guilty of reckless homicide and child neglect in the death of their 9-month-old daughter. Allyson Bergmann became ill May 28, 1984, and her parents treated her with prayers, fasting, and invocations of scripture. Allyson died eleven days later from bacterial meningitis. Indiana, like Florida, recognizes a religious-belief exception to the statute pertaining to child neglect. The Bergmanns appealed their conviction on the basis of this exception, but the appellate judge let the conviction stand, arguing that the religious-belief defense was a question of fact for the jury to decide.

In contrast, in 1990 a Minnesota judge ruled that a Christian Scientist couple could not be prosecuted for manslaughter in the death of a diabetic 11-year-old boy who was the wife's natural son and the husband's stepson. The judge here cited the state law on child neglect that excepted religious treatment.

In a widely publicized recent [as of 1993] Massachusetts case, David and Ginger Twitchell were found guilty of involuntary manslaughter in the 1990 death of their 2 1/2-year-old son Robyn. When Robyn became ill in 1986, his parents treated him solely with prayers. Five days later, he died of a bowel obstruction. Although the Twitchells could have received up to 20 years in prison, the judge placed them on ten years' probation. They were also ordered to take their three remaining sons in for periodic medical checkups with a licensed pediatrician.

In Florida, a Christian Scientist husband and wife received probation for an April 1989 conviction of third-degree murder in not providing medical treatment for their diabetic 7-year-old daughter. But recently [as of 1993] the Florida Supreme Court reversed their conviction, stating that the religious treatment exception was too vague.

This decision will likely affect the convictions of Charles and Merilee Myers, members of a religious sect that shuns doctors. They were given five years' probation in 1991 for medical neglect of their 16-year-old son who did not die from what doctors diagnosed as a near-fatal heart tumor. "Adults are free to choose martyrdom," the prosecuting attorney said. "Children cannot have it thrust upon them."

In August 1989, a Santa Rosa, California, jury acquitted two Christian Scientists of involuntary manslaughter in the meningitis death of their 15-month-old daughter, but convicted them of child endangerment. However, a Los Angeles judge in February 1990 acquitted another Christian Scientist couple of involuntary manslaughter for the meningitis death of their toddler son for insufficient evidence.

A New Trend in Court-Ordered Treatment

Several other cases indicate that the trend in some states is to order medical treatment over a parent's religious objections even where there is no life-threatening condition.

In the 1972 case of *Re Karwath*, an Iowa court held that a juvenile court acted properly when it ordered surgical removal of the tonsils and adenoids of three children in the state's care despite the father's religious objections. The father wanted the surgery to be a last resort after medication and chiropractics had been used. According to the medical testimony, the children

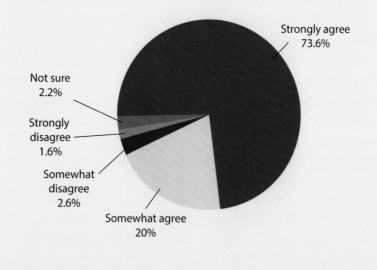

AMERICANS' VIEWS ON PARENTAL RIGHTS

In general, parents have the constitutional right to make decisions for their children without governmental interference unless there is proof of abuse or neglect. Do you agree or disagree with this view of parental rights?

Strongly agree
73.6%

Not sure
2.2%

Strongly
disagree
1.6%

Somewhat
disagree
2.6%

Somewhat agree
20%

Taken from: Zogby Poll, August 27–30, 2010.

were suffering from middle-ear infections that "could possibly lead to loss of hearing and rheumatic fever." The oldest child had missed several days of school because of his ear problems and concern over this inattendance weighed heavily in the court's ruling.

In a 1972 New York case, a family court judge ordered doctors to perform what was characterized as "risky" surgery on a 15-year-old whose face and neck had been disfigured by a non-fatal, incurable disease. Here again the judge concluded that non-emergency surgery can be ordered over parental religious objections because of the state interest involved in compulsory education. The 15-year-old had not been attending school because of his disfigurement.

In California, a court ordered corrective surgery for a 6-year-old boy born with clubfeet. The boy's Laotian-born parents had opposed the surgery because they believed that the boy's clubfeet was a curse inflicted on them by the spirits. The U.S. Supreme Court in 1990 refused to overturn the lower court's ruling that authorized the surgery. Nonetheless, despite the court order, no hospital has agreed to perform the operation without parental consent.

In Connecticut, in 1990, a 7-year-old girl born with rheumatoid arthritis was taken from her mother because her mother, a Chinese immigrant named Juliet Cheng, had been treating her daughter Shirley with acupuncture, herbal potions, and other non-Western medical treatments. The mother had initially sought help from an American doctor who prescribed aspirin for the then 11-month-old girl, but the mother said the treatment didn't help. Doctors at Newington Children's Hospital in Poughkeepsie, New York, told Cheng that Shirley needed surgery or she would never walk again. When Cheng refused, the hospital persuaded the State Department of Children and Youth Services to take custody of the child. After five months, however, the state Department relinquished custody to the mother after two of the three doctors on the court-approved panel had examined the girl and recommended against the surgery.

The State's Position

The notion *parens patriae* is the fundamental principle behind this case law. It means "father of the country" and it denotes the state's role as a sovereign guardian over "persons under disability." It ultimately places the power in the state government to determine to what extent it will act to protect the interests of "its" children. Thus, the state is always the backstop and referee behind every parent. The state is the one that prescribes a legal duty to those charged with the care of a child to provide that child with medical attention. The parents are prosecuted for breaching this duty, and religious freedom is involved only parenthetically as a possible argument against state intrusion.

"Acting to guard the general interest in the youth's well-being, the state as *parens patriae* may restrict the parent's control by requiring school attendance, regulating or prohibiting the child's labor, and in many other ways. Its authority is not nullified merely because the parent grounds his claim to control the child's course of conduct on religion or conscience" [*com v. Barnhart*].

But the million-dollar question is what course of treatment will guarantee a child's well-being?

The Absence of Certainty

Medical testimony is crucial in these cases. The child's death has to be seen as the result of the parents' failure to get medical attention. Doctors cite statistics on the child's chances of survival based on the stage the disease is in when treatment is begun. For example, in the Pennsylvania *Barnhart* case, a doctor testified that the child's chance of surviving the cancerous tumor was 95 percent if the cancer was discovered at an early stage, 85 percent if the tumor had spread locally, and so forth.

Yet, even if true, what do these statistics mean? The 5 percent who don't survive even when the cancer is discovered at an early stage die for a variety of reasons. The treatment may fail to cure the cancer or the treatment itself may kill them. Who can tell whether the Barnhart child falls in the 95 percent or the 5 percent? The state certainly can't know.

The scientifically naive believe that there is truth in science. They see medicine as equivalent to mathematics where 2 plus 2 always equals 4 and, therefore, when a doctor diagnoses a heart tumor as "fatal," it will cause death 100 percent of the time. But medicine is not a logical system; it exists in the empirical world of complex human organisms. When the court officials order that the child be treated and the child dies, hasn't the child in this situation also had "martyrdom" thrust upon him?

Science, particularly medicine, is experimental, which means no particular result is predictable with 100 percent accuracy. The U.S. Government Office of Technology Assessment reports that 80 to 90 percent of doctors' treatment methods are not based on scientifically proven principles and, consequently, the results are not guaranteed reproducible. Childhood vaccinations that were supposed to wipe out illnesses are themselves responsible for causing severe health problems and even death in a small minority of children. According to the California Department of Health Services, the risk of dying or developing brain damage from the pertussis vaccine is estimated to be one in 100,000, and the chance of developing paralysis from the polio vaccine is one in 500,000.

There are also other complicating factors. Studies show the high risk involved in medical treatment, for example, of misdiagnosis, and that one out of five people entering a hospital leaves with a condition he didn't have when he entered.

The Unfair Treatment of Parents

David and Ginger Twitchell, the Massachusetts Christian Scientists convicted of involuntary manslaughter, had thought their son was sick with the flu. He had felt well enough to go outside and play the day before he died. After the trial was over, David Twitchell told reporters that he and his wife "will try to obey the judge's instructions," but he added that he was "having trouble figuring out whose judgment is going to decide exactly when a problem is serious and not just a cold." He also stated that he didn't believe a regular checkup would have saved his son's life.

In every one of these cases, the state acts under the mistaken notion that it can accomplish what it sets out to accomplish: the child's well-being. Further, if parents are to be criminally liable, then the government, as *parens patriae*, when it fails to cure the child, should also be liable to criminal prosecution. But the truth is that in every case the parents are being held liable because their chosen course of treatment failed to cure their children. It was the illness itself—whether bowel obstruction, meningitis, cancer, diabetes, or whatever—that killed the child. Under the government's own logic, state officials who mandate that modern medicine be used should also be held guilty when modern medicine fails.

A different standard is being applied to the parents than to the state in these cases that involve a failure to cure. These are not cases of medical malpractice or parental abuse where the doctors or parents contribute to causing the child's death by an act of poisoning, starvation, administration of the wrong medication, or some other kind of physical abuse. When the parents do their very best for their children and the children die, the parents are held responsible for their failure to cure the child. But when the doctors do their very best for a child and the child dies, the doctors are not held responsible for their failure to cure the child. This results in an unfair, inequitable treatment of the parents.

A Fair and Equitable Standard

To apply the state laws to everyone equally and to eliminate this unfair double standard, the legal system has two choices. The system can prosecute parents, government officials, and doctors alike when their mandated course of treatment fails to cure the child. The doctor who follows the medically accepted treatment of chemotherapy for cancer and cures his patient won't be prosecuted. The doctor who follows the same course of treatment but fails to cure his patient will be prosecuted as well as the government official who authorized the treatment. Of course, if officials and doctors are more successful at curing cancer, meningitis, and other diseases than parents are, the percentage of doctors and officials being prosecuted would be less than the percentage of parents being prosecuted.

The other option, which is supported by the Constitution's First Amendment, is for the members of the legal community to realize that even though science has become enormously successful, disease and other maladies can never be perfectly controlled by any judge, doctor, parent, or legislature. Parents should be accorded the same immunity from prosecution when their cures fail as doctors are in the same circumstances. And, then, parents will be free to pursue the course of treatment they choose without state intrusion.

The attitude of state judicial and legislative systems is threatening the preservation of freedom. State officials attempt to ascribe a certainty to science and medicine that simply is impossible to achieve. By science's nature, there can be no certainty for treating a particular sick child. It is time to eliminate the double standard for parents and doctors.

> "Children deserve medical care and parents who refuse medical care in cases such as these have no right to allow their children to die without the care and treatments."

Religious Freedom Does Not Allow a Parent to Refuse Medical Treatment for a Child

R. Albert Mohler Jr.

In the following viewpoint, R. Albert Mohler Jr. argues that the right to religious freedom does not allow parents to decide to deny their children urgently needed medical treatments. Mohler contends that in cases where children are being denied necessary medical treatment, the state is justified in stepping in to protect the health and life of the child. Mohler cautions that parental rights should be respected and upheld generally, but in this situation he claims there is no social or religious justification for allowing parents the freedom to deny children needed care. Mohler is president of The Southern Baptist Theological Seminary, the flagship school of the Southern Baptist Convention and one of the world's biggest seminaries.

New Court Cases Highlight Tragic Deaths

Recent cases involving parents who claim a religious reason to refuse medical treatment for children have cast this issue back into the public square—and right into the headlines.

The cases draw immediate attention for good reason. Each case involves a sick or injured child, and in each case at least one parent refuses to allow needed medical treatments, claiming either a reliance upon divine healing, a resignation to the divine will, a medical practice specific to the religious tradition, or some particular objection to a specific medical treatment (such as a blood transfusion) or to all medical interventions.

Each case involves what appears to be conflicting interests—the parental right to determine the raising of children and the state's interest in protecting the health and welfare of all citizens, including minors. All of these cases are tortuous in some sense, and some are deeply tragic.

In the case of Daniel Hauser, a 13-year-old Minnesota boy with Hodgkin's lymphoma, the issue is the fact that his mother, Colleen Hauser, has defied legal authorities and is believed to have taken him to Mexico for non-traditional treatments for his cancer. The Hausers believe in medical practices based on Native American traditions. After an emotional appeal from the boy's father, the mother and son returned Memorial Day to Minnesota, where he will now receive treatment directed by pediatric oncologists. There is good reason to hope that the chemotherapy will be successful in the case of this treatable cancer.

In another highly publicized case, Leilani Neumann of Wausau, Wisconsin was convicted last week of second-degree reckless homicide in the death of her 11-year-old daughter, Madeline Kara Neumann. Mrs. Neumann refused to allow medical treatment for her daughter's diabetes, and the girl died. The mother claimed a belief in faith healing as her rationale for refusing medical treatment for her daughter. According to medical authorities who testified at the trial, insulin and fluids would have kept the girl alive. Mrs. Neumann now awaits sentencing.

Another recent case involves a 16-year-old boy in Oregon who died a painful death when his parents refused medical treatment for what started out as a simple urinary tract infection. Citing a belief in faith healing, his parents substituted prayer for medical treatment. According to medical authorities, the boy's death was easily preventable. As these cases make clear, the headlines draw attention for good reason—children deserve medical care and parents who refuse medical care in cases such as these have no right to allow their children to die without the care and treatments.

The State Should Protect Children's Right to Medical Care, Say Americans

And, amazingly enough, there is a strong moral consensus in this country that children deserve medical care and that the state has the obligation to intervene in such cases. This consensus includes both political liberals and conservatives and includes the vast majority of Americans regardless of religious conviction. Though there are important legal issues at stake, a broad consensus exists on this narrowly-defined question. In cases like those recounted above, there is no outcry against state intervention from Christian conservatives or from secular liberals.

The 1944 U.S. Supreme Court decision *Prince v. Massachusetts* set parameters that continue today. In that case, the Court acknowledged the rights of parents as fundamental. In an important statement the court expressed this right: "It is cardinal with us that the custody, care and nurture of the child reside first in the parents, whose primary function and freedom include preparation for obligations the state can neither supply nor hinder [*Pierce v. Society of Sisters*, supra.]. And it is in recognition of this that these decisions have respected the private realm of family life which the state cannot enter."

The Limits of Religious Freedom

The limits of religious freedom would not be hard to understand if adult interests were being compromised. No legislature has enacted religious defenses to crimes against adults.

The bottom line is that children are helpless and that parents have custody of them. Society must require parents to provide children with the necessities of life regardless of their religious beliefs.

Rita Swan, "Letting Children Die for the Faith,"
Free Inquiry, *Winter 1998.*

But the Court also found that there were issues of the welfare of a child that could draw state authorities into this "private realm." Specifically, "The right to practice religion freely does not include liberty to expose the community or the child to communicable disease or the latter to ill health or death."

As a parent, I respect this point. I cannot imagine denying my child any needed medical treatment or defending the right of others to do the same, whether claiming religious liberty or parental freedom for the care and nurture of the child.

I would defend the duty of the state to intervene in these cases, and I am thankful for the broad consensus that stands behind this duty.

I am not without concerns. Given the power of government and the reach of the state into almost all areas of life, the danger exists that the state could seek to expand this duty into other decisions related to education, discipline, and nurture—the very issues acknowledged by the Court in *Prince v. Massachusetts* to "reside first in the parents." Yet, vigilance on those questions is the price that must be paid, lest more children be added to the list of those who die or are endangered by parents who claim a religious right to deny their child urgently needed medical

Colleen Hauser arrives for a hearing at the Brown County Courthouse in 2009 in New Ulm, Minnesota. Hauser faced legal trouble after trying to deny cancer treatment for her thirteen-year-old son Daniel. © Jim Mone/Associated Press.

treatment. As adults, parents have the right to refuse medical treatment for themselves. They do not have the right to refuse urgently needed medical treatments for their children.

The Bible Does Not Prohibit Medical Treatment

As a Christian theologian, my concern is also directed to those who oppose medical treatment on what are claimed as biblical grounds. The Bible never commands any refusal of legitimate medical treatment. I am unspeakably thankful for modern medicine, for antibiotics and anesthesia and chemotherapy and dialysis and diagnostics. The list goes on and on. There is no Christian prohibition against legitimate medical treatment. I believe that God heals, that we should pray for healing in Christ's name, and that our lives are in God's hands. I believe that all healing comes ultimately from God, but that He has given us the blessings of medicine for the alleviation of much suffering and the treatment of disease. There is no conflict here.

There are serious issues of medical ethics in the case of some treatments, even as there are excruciating dilemmas that confront physicians, patients, and parents. Those must be acknowledged, but they are not the issues at stake in these cases.

In these cases I advise what the great Reformer Martin Luther advised—take your medicine and put your trust in God. For parents, this means to give your child the best care that modern medicine can offer, and to entrust your precious child to God and to God alone.

> *"We lost our only son Matthew as a result of our religious beliefs regarding medical care."*

A Parent Recounts Her Decision to Refuse Medical Treatment for Religious Reasons

Personal Narrative

Rita Swan

In the following viewpoint Rita Swan recounts her experience as a member of the Christian Science church, during which time she and her husband followed the teachings of the church and relied on prayer rather than medical care to cure their ill child, losing their son to likely treatable meningitis. Having since left the church, Swan claims that numerous child deaths result from the failure of parents within faith-healing communities to seek necessary medical treatment. She contends that medical neglect leads to other problems besides death, but that state laws support the rights of parents in many instances to deny their children proper medical care. Swan now believes that children have the right to medical care

Rita Swan, "When Faith Fails Children: Religion-Based Neglect: Pervasive, Deadly . . . and Legal?," *The Humanist*, November–December 2000, pp. 11–16. Copyright © 2000 by Rita Swan. All rights reserved. Reproduced by permission.

and that this right should be enshrined in law. Swan is president of Children's Healthcare Is a Legal Duty, Inc. (CHILD), a membership organization founded to protect children from religion-based medical neglect.

My husband Douglas and I were devout, lifelong Christian Scientists until 1977 when we lost our only son Matthew as a result of our religious beliefs regarding medical care. It's hard for most people to understand this. It's hard for many to grasp how parents could watch a beloved child suffer, yet not call a doctor. I need to begin, therefore, by describing the pressures involved.

The Beliefs of Christian Scientists

The First Church of Christ, Scientist, founded in the late nineteenth century by Mary Baker Eddy, teaches that all disease is caused by sin. As little Matthew lay helpless with a raging fever, his body and bedding soaked with perspiration, the Christian Science practitioners told us that our negative feelings were making our baby sick. Our doubts, fears, lack of gratitude to them, and problems with relatives were the sins causing Matthew's illness.

Christian Science theology had trained us to believe that physicians don't really heal—at best, they only relieve symptoms; the underlying cause of the disease remains a moral problem that God alone can solve. Furthermore, this church doesn't allow its practitioners to give spiritual treatments to those who voluntarily go to a physician. Such a rule, as contrasted with the teachings of most other religious denominations, instructs that God and a doctor are mutually exclusive alternatives.

The Christian Science church also opposes medical diagnosis as much as it does medical treatment. Because of this, my husband and I had no way of acquiring rational information about Matthew's illness without breaking church rules. We wanted relief for our baby and considered taking him to a doctor, but we were terrified that the doctor wouldn't be able to treat the disease, which was a mystery to us, and then we'd have no way to resume the Christian Science healing. Thus, if we made the wrong decision, we could find ourselves bereft of help from both medical science and God.

On the twelfth day of his illness, however, a path of action seemed to open for us. The practitioner told us that Matthew might have a broken bone and that the Christian Science church does allow members to go to doctors to have bones set. Immediately we took Matthew to a hospital. As I walked in with our nearly dead baby in my arms, I asked the staff to check him for only the broken bone. But later, when we phoned our practitioner from the hospital, expecting her to continue praying for Matthew, she indignantly rejected us, saying that she had "seen all along" we were lacking in faith.

Our baby was diagnosed with h-flu meningitis, which has been routinely treated with antibiotics since the 1940s and is vaccine-preventable today. The doctors explained to us how the disease had caused the symptoms we had seen. That's when we realized that the very things the Christian Science practitioners had insisted were signs the religious treatments were working were, in fact, signs of impending disaster. (For example, one practitioner, who observed Matthew's convulsions, said he might be "gritting his teeth" because he was "planning some great achievement.")

Matthew lived a week longer in intensive care on a respirator and then died. Immediately afterwards, my husband and I left the Christian Science church. . . .

Child Deaths in Faith-Healing Communities

Pediatrician Seth M. Asser and I conducted the largest study ever done on child fatalities in faith-healing sects and published our results in the April 1998 issue of *Pediatrics*. We analyzed the deaths which occurred between 1975 and 1995 of 200 U.S. children, who were associated with eighteen different religious sects that object to medical care. We were able to obtain documentation on 172 of these cases sufficient to conclude that medical care was withheld on religious grounds. And of those 172 children, 140 of them would have had a 90 percent or better probability of survival if adequate medical care had been provided in a timely way.

Unexpectedly, our work immediately served as a catalyst for an important new discovery. Shortly after our results were published, public officials in Oregon disclosed to the media that a large number of children from a Followers of Christ congregation near Oregon City had died. Seventy-eight children were found to be buried in a cemetery owned by this church. Another dozen Followers of Christ children died near Caldwell, Idaho, over a twenty-year span.

None of these ninety children was included in our *Pediatrics* study. In fact, when we did our research we hadn't even heard of the Followers of Christ. Yet these children had been dying year after year, from 1955 through 1998, and nobody outside the group had any real idea.

In the light of this and other information we've acquired since our study, we believe that the numerous deaths across the nation known to us are but a small fraction of the actual total. This may be especially true where coroners have failed to do autopsies in such cases. And the religious groups tend to keep the facts to themselves.

The Consequences of Medical Neglect

The Christian Science church in particular has admitted to its lack of internal accountability and recordkeeping. Its officials have sworn under oath that the Christian Science church has no "supervisory control" over its practitioners, that it doesn't "ever evaluate a practitioner's judgment about the condition of sick children," that it has no training, workshops, or meetings for practitioners that "include any discussion on how to evaluate the seriousness of a child's condition," that it has never "named the death of a child as a grounds for revoking a practitioner's listing," and that it keeps no records on children who die while receiving Christian Science prayer treatments.

Death isn't the only consequence of religiously motivated medical neglect. Untold numbers more, who grew up in homes with parents who had religious objections to medical care, have suffered needless fear and pain or have become permanently disabled. Illnesses and injuries left untreated can produce a host of outcomes. For example, some CHILD [Children's Healthcare Is a Legal Duty, Inc.] members can trace hearing loss to such neglect. And one became profoundly deaf at age seven after a series of ear infections for which her Christian Science parents wouldn't secure medical treatment.

Thousands of children aren't inoculated against communicable diseases because of their parents' religious objections. The Christian Science church has told its practitioners and nurses not to report contagious diseases to their state and has discouraged them from reporting cases of sick children without medical care to protection services agencies. Though the church does advise parents to report suspected communicable diseases to public health departments, church members aren't likely to "suspect" a communicable disease when their theology teaches them that disease is an illusion, rendering them ignorant of disease symptoms.

Outbreaks of contagious disease in groups with religious objections to medical care are no surprise. An epidemic of polio in 1972 at a Christian Science boarding school in Connecticut left eleven children paralyzed. Health authorities didn't learn of the outbreak until twenty days after the first student became ill. In Philadelphia, Pennsylvania, during February and March 1991, 492 cases of measles, resulting in six deaths, occurred among the children of the Faith Tabernacle Congregation and the First Century Gospel Church.

Contagious diseases can also spread to those outside faith-healing sects. For example, in 1982, nine-year-old Debra Kupsch contracted diphtheria at a Christian Science camp in Colorado, then traveled on a bus with a number of other unvaccinated children to Wisconsin where she died. The state of Wisconsin then had to track down and test all the children and adults she had come into contact with. In 1985, one child whose parents had claimed a religious exemption from state-required immunizations became the index patient for a measles outbreak that ripped through the Blackfeet Indian Reservation near Glacier National Park in Montana, affecting 137 people. In 1994, at the Principia Christian Science parochial schools in the St. Louis, Missouri, area, an outbreak of measles spread to more than 200 children, including many outside the Christian Science community. It was the nation's largest measles outbreak since 1992 and cost St. Louis County taxpayers over $100,000.

The Right to Religious Freedom

Religious freedom, [of] course, is a precious right, but our courts have never ruled that the First Amendment includes a right to deprive a child of preventive, therapeutic, or diagnostic health care. Indeed, they have issued opinions in the opposite direction. Over a half century ago, in 1944, the U. S. Supreme Court ruled in *Prince v. Massachusetts*:

> The right to practice religion freely does not include liberty to expose the community or child to communicable disease, or the latter to ill health or death. . . . Parents may be free to become martyrs themselves. But it does not follow they are free, in identical circumstances, to make martyrs of their children before they have reached the age of full and legal discretion when they can make that choice for themselves.

Given this clear ruling on the limitations of religious freedom and given the fact that many parents have been prosecuted and convicted for withholding lifesaving medical care on religious grounds, one may wonder what more needs to be done. Unfortunately, state and federal legislatures have given parents religious rights to endanger their children. Consider the following issues.

Exemptions from preventive and diagnostic measures. Right now, forty-eight states have religious exemptions from immunizations; Mississippi and West Virginia are the only ones that require all children to be immunized without exception for religious belief. The majority of states have religious exemptions from metabolic testing of newborns. Such tests detect disorders that will cause mental retardation and other disabilities unless treated.

Sometimes the treatment is simple dietary control until the child's body is able to metabolize protein. Iowa, Minnesota, Colorado, and Michigan have religious exemptions from prophylactic eyedrops for newborns; the eyedrops prevent blindness of infants who have been infected with venereal diseases carried by their mothers. Delaware, Illinois, Kansas, Maine, Massachusetts, New Jersey, and Rhode Island have religious exemptions from screening children for lead poisoning.

California, Colorado, Michigan, Minnesota, and Ohio statutes offer religious exemptions from physical examinations of school children. California, Connecticut, New Jersey, and West Virginia have a religious exemption from hearing tests for newborns. California, Colorado, Massachusetts, Michigan, Minnesota, and Ohio have statutes excusing students with religious objections from even studying about disease in school. And California has a religious exemption from tuberculosis testing of public school teachers.

Exemptions from providing care. Forty-one states have religious exemptions from child abuse or neglect charges. Thirty-one states allow a religious defense to a criminal charge. States with a religious defense to the most serious crimes against children include: Iowa and Ohio, with religious defenses to manslaughter; Delaware and West Virginia, with religious defenses to the murder of a child; and Arkansas, with a religious defense to capital murder. States with a religious defense to child endangerment, criminal abuse or neglect, and cruelty to children include Alabama, Colorado, Delaware, Georgia, Idaho, Indiana, Iowa, Kansas, Louisiana, Maine, Minnesota, Missouri, Nevada, New Hampshire, New Jersey, New York, Ohio, Oklahoma, South Carolina, Tennessee, Texas, Utah, Virginia, West Virginia, and Wisconsin. Florida's religious exemption appears only in the juvenile code but has been ruled a defense to felony abuse charges. States with a religious-exemption-to-nonsupport charge against deadbeat parents include Alaska, California, Idaho, Missouri, and South Dakota.

Several exemption statutes, both in the civil and criminal codes, have ambiguities that may make them merely a statement of one's right to pray rather than a right to withhold necessary medical care from a child. Prosecutors have sometimes filed criminal charges and won convictions under chapters of the code that don't have religious exemptions. Nevertheless, some church officials have continued to advise members that the exemption laws confer the right to withhold medical care no matter how sick the child is and even that the laws were passed because legislators understood prayer to be as effective as medicine....

The Rights of Children

Why, in the twenty-first century, is this situation allowed to continue? I think it's because the United States remains reluctant to fully acknowledge children as rights-bearing persons. The public and its lawmakers aren't ready to give children a constitutional right to health care. While states do require parents to provide their children with the necessities of life, they don't always require that children receive adequate health care. And every state, at one time or another, has passed laws allowing parents to withhold on religious grounds some forms of medical treatment.

Religious exemption laws create two classes of children. One is entitled to preventive, diagnostic, and therapeutic health care because their parents have a legal duty to provide it. The other—those in faith-healing sects—have no right to immunizations, prophylactic eyedrops, or health screenings and, depending on the reach of the religious defense in the criminal code, no right to medical care for illnesses unless and until a state agency becomes aware of their needs and obtains care by court order.

In our view, religious exemptions from the duties of care are an unconstitutional violation of the rights of children and not a valid act of legislative discretion. Such exemptions discriminate against a class of children, depriving them of their Fourteenth Amendment right to equal protection under the laws, and give a preference and an endorsement to a religious practice, violating the establishment clause of the First Amendment. As mentioned above, the U.S. Supreme Court ruled over fifty years ago in *Prince* that First Amendment rights to religious freedom don't include depriving children of needed medical care. What is still urgently needed, however, is a federal court ruling that religious exemptions from child health care laws are themselves unconstitutional.

Children aren't property. Their right to life and health should take precedence over their parents' right to practice religion. Parents have every right to pray, of course. Parents have rights to cultural and religious practices that may differ from the prevailing community standards unless they present a specific threat to a child's health or welfare. Parents have rights to privacy in many childrearing decisions beyond the legitimate concern of the state. But parents should also do everything in their power to protect the life and health of their children.

> "By stealing the rights of fit parents to care for their own children, the brick and mortar that sustains the wall protecting families from government intrusion is being destroyed."

Medicine, Minors, and Parents: Diminishing Parental Rights in Medicine

Mary Summa

In the following viewpoint, Mary Summa argues that parental rights are under assault in the United States. Summa contends that although traditionally the US Supreme Court has recognized the rights of parents to make decisions about their children, in recent decades the courts have chipped away at parental authority, especially in the area of medical care. Summa claims that new laws have mandated health care without parental consent and shut out parents from accessing their child's health care records. Summa argues that children need to be protected from this state intervention and parental rights need to be strengthened. Summa is an attorney in Charlotte, North Carolina.

Imagine these scenarios: Jane is 15 years old. She has had sexual relations with her boyfriend and has contracted the deadly AIDS virus. She is being treated for the disease, although there is no cure. Her parents were not notified and were not asked for consent. They have no legal right to know. Susan is 12 years old and has asked for and received the Gardasil vaccination without her parents' knowledge or consent. She experiences seizures from the vaccine, but her parents are unable to adequately help her because they do not know the cause of the seizures. They are not allowed to access to Susan's medical records.

Nationwide, 31 states, including North Carolina, explicitly allow children to be tested and treated for the deadly AIDS virus without the knowledge or consent of their parents.

In California, a law, which went into effect January 1, 2012, authorizes girls as young as 12 years old to obtain the HPV vaccine without their parents' knowledge or consent, despite a report revealing that nationwide, between September 1, 2010 and September 15, 2011, 26 girls died from the vaccine.

Proponents of these laws argue that it is in the child's "best interest" to take this authority away from parents and give it to "professionals" to guide children in such life and death decisions.

That is simply nonsense. These laws are the latest assault on the family in a battle that has been waged against it for the latter half of the 20th Century and into the 21st. By stealing the rights of fit parents to care for their own children, the brick and mortar that sustains the wall protecting families from government intrusion is being destroyed. Once that wall falls, government control of children is not far behind.

Those who are really interested in the well-being of children and freedom should demand that parents be returned their God-given fundamental right to care for their own children.

Foundational Parental Rights

God, as the creator of all things, is the author of legitimate authority. Parents are the stewards of that authority with the God-given right to make decisions on behalf of their children. John Locke, the 17th Century English philosopher, understood parental rights to include the right to rule over one's children and to rear them as parents deem appropriate. This right cannot be usurped by society or a parent's own child.

This right, as adopted into English common law, includes the right to custody, the right to raise a child in a particular faith, the right to make education and health care choices, and the right to access a child's medical and educational records. This right, according to the English jurist, William Blackstone, emanates from a parent's duty to provide for the maintenance of his children and is considered a fundamental right.

Protecting Parental Rights

Legally, minors lack the competence to make decisions regarding their upbringing, education, and medical care. Traditionally, in education, the U.S. Supreme Court has respected and protected parental rights, reinforcing the legal presumption that parents act in their children's best interest. In 1923, in 1925, and in 1972, the Court upheld the right and responsibility of parents to educate their own children without the meddling hand of government. Similarly, the Court has upheld the fundamental right of parents to control the custody and visitation of their children. In 2000, the Court struck down a Washington State statute that authorized the court to grant visitation rights "to any person" if the judge believed it was in the "best interest of the child."

In 1979, the Court upheld the rights of parents to admit their child into a mental health facility. In *Parham v. J.R.*, the Court recognized that the parent's natural bond with his or her child leads the parent to act in that child's best interest, and absent neglect or abuse, a parent should "retain a substantial—if not dominant role in the decision." A parent's authority is not absolute, according to the Court, but the belief that government authority should supersede parental authority for all parents

Protestors participate in a pro-life rally during the 2012 Democratic National Convention. Some believe that parental rights, including abortion, are under assault in the United States. © Robyn Beck/AFP/Getty Images.

simply because of bad parenting by the few is "repugnant to the American tradition."

In contrast, in the area of reproductive "rights," the Court has stolen from fit parents the absolute right to control the behavior of their children. While the Court has upheld state laws requiring parental consent or parental notice for abortions, the minor can petition the court to bypass the parents. In effect, the state, not fit parents, have the ultimate authority to decide whether a minor can obtain an abortion.

Lower courts, beginning in the late 1990s, started abandoning parental rights:

- In 1995 the First U.S. Circuit Court of Appeals denied to parents the right to be notified or remove their children from a sexually explicit presentation in a public school assembly.

- In 1998, a federal appeals court refused to hear a case involving parents objecting to the distribution of condoms on school property without parental consent. The court sided with the school district claiming that it was "promoting public health."

- In 2005, the Ninth U.S. Circuit Court of Appeals upheld the right of schools to distribute intrusive values surveys. In refusing to hear a case brought by parents challenging the school district, the court stated that parental rights "do not extend beyond the threshold of the school door."

- In 2008, a federal appeals court found that parents who object on moral grounds to a particular portion of a school curriculum do not have the right to remove their child from the program or even know about it in advance.

Government Seizes Parental Authority

In most states, after reaching 18, a child is considered legally independent from their parents, and is legally responsible for his own actions and care. Many states have emancipated minors based on the "status" of the minor, including marriage, military service, or court order. In recent years, states have expanded "status" emancipation to include pregnancy, living with a child, living apart from their parents and financially independent, or a victim of sexual assault or abuse.

In recent years, creating a child's right to privacy, the U.S. Supreme Court has allowed minors to consent to various "services," namely, abortion and contraceptives. Following suit, states have allowed minor consent to these "services," plus testing and treatment for venereal disease (including HIV), prenatal care, mental health, and alcohol and drug abuse. Specifically:

- 46 states have specific laws allowing minors to consent to contraceptives.
- 21 states and the District of Columbia allow all minors to receive contraceptives without parental consent or notification.
- 25 states allow minors to consent to contraceptive services under certain circumstances.

According to the Guttmacher Institute, as of December 2012, North Dakota, Ohio, Rhode Island, and Wisconsin do not have specific statutory language authorizing minor consent for contraceptives. All four states, however, provide contraceptives without parental consent in facilities funded by Medicaid or Title X of the Health Care Services Act, including many Planned Parenthood facilities. Although there have been several attempts in Congress to require parental consent for contraceptives provided by Title X funds, all attempts have failed. Medicaid's expansion under Obamacare will rob even more parents of their right to consent to contraceptives given to their children.

In 2011, in an attempt to circumvent parental authority, a new program, called CATCH, was launched in New York City public schools. Through this program, "morning-after pills" and DepoProvera (an injectable contraceptive) were dispensed to children without parental consent or knowledge. Reportedly, the school district's actions prompted one school staffer to ask, "Why in the world should a school district, which can't give out a Tylenol without parent consent, be allowed to dispense drugs with far more serious possible side effects, such as blood clots and hypertension?"

All 50 states and the District of Columbia allow minors to consent to services involving sexually transmitted infections, although 11 of these states require that a minor be of a certain age to consent. Thirty-one states, including North Carolina, include

HIV in the list of sexually transmitted diseases for which a minor can consent to testing and/or treatment. Only 18 states allow physicians to notify parents that their child is seeking or receiving treatment. Only in Iowa are physicians required to notify a parent of a positive HIV result.

By 2000, 44 states and the District of Columbia had enacted laws or policies that took from parents the right to consent to drug or alcohol treatment for their child, and 20 states had taken that right from parents regarding outpatient mental health services. At least one state allows minors to consent to sterilization. North Carolina allows children to consent to mental health, drug and alcohol treatment but, thankfully, does not allow minors to be sterilized without parental consent.

"Mature Minor" Laws

In recent years, a few states have turned parental authority over to the courts. "Mature minor" statutes give judges the authority to decide if a minor is "sufficiently" mature to understand the consequences and risks of certain decisions, including medical decisions. The minor's age, capability of giving informed consent, whether the treatment is beneficial, the risk of the treatment, and whether the treatment is within established medical protocols are considered. Using the "mature minor" doctrine, the U.S. Supreme Court has required a judicial bypass for state statutes authorizing parental notification or consent for abortion.

Parens Patriae and Gardasil

Parental rights are based on the belief that parents act in the best interest of their child. The right, however, is not absolute. When a parent fails to provide shelter, food, clothing, certain medical care, or basic needs, the state can step in and provide those essentials for the child and, possibly, remove the child from the parent's custody. This authority, based on the state's obligation to protect life, is called the *Parens Patriae* Doctrine, and means "parent of the nation." Conceptually derived from English common law, the doctrine has been significantly expanded in American law in a number of legal areas, including medical care.

Parens Patriae has been used to impose health mandates on the public. As early as 1905, the Supreme Court upheld the right of municipalities to require vaccinations. In the 20th Century, states used the *Parens Patriae* doctrine to require vaccinations for airborne diseases including diphtheria, rubella, polio, and measles.

Considering the easy transmission of these illnesses through the air or by contact, and the seriousness of these illnesses, few argue that this application of the *Parens Patriae* doctrine is unjustified, especially when state statutes provide a religious, medical, or philosophical exemption. In recent years, however, two states and the District of Columbia have used the doctrine as their legal spear to require girls as young as 12 years old to receive Gardasil, a vaccination designed to protect against contracting the human papilloma virus (HPV), which is transmitted mainly by sexual activity, including skin to skin contact. In 2007, Texas Governor Rick Perry issued an executive order requiring all 6th grade girls to obtain Gardasil. The public viewed Perry's actions as a power grab that trampled parental rights. Approximately 60 state legislators asked Perry to rescind his order. He refused, and within two months, the Texas Legislature nullified the order by an overwhelming vote in both houses of the State Legislature.

In Virginia, in 2007, the legislature enacted a law similar to Perry's executive order. A 2012 report by two Canadian researchers found that possible side effects of the drug include:

> death, convulsions, paraesthesia, paralysis, Guillain-Barre syndrome, transverse myelitis, facial palsy, chronic fatigue syndrome, anaphylaxis, autoimmune disorders, deep vein thrombosis, pulmonary embolisms and cervical cancers.

Responding to this report, in February 2012, the Virginia House of Delegates voted to repeal the Gardasil law. Later that month, the Virginia Senate returned the bill to committee where

The Importance of Parents

By deciding that the child's decision should be respected over the parents' decision, physicians are replacing the parents' judgment that the decision should be overridden with their judgment that the child's decision should be respected. To do so makes this less an issue of respecting the child's autonomy, and more about deciding who knows what is best for the child. In general, parents are the better judge as they have a more vested interest in their child's well-being and are responsible for the day-to-day decisions of child-rearing. It behooves physicians to be humble as they are neither able nor willing to take over this daily function.

Lainie Friedman Ross, "Health Care Decision-making by Children—Is It in Their Best Interest?," Hastings Center Report, vol. 27, no. 6, November/December 1997.

it will sit until the 2013 legislative session. To date, only Virginia and the District of Columbia mandate the Gardasil vaccination as a prerequisite for school admission for 6th grade girls.

In 2008, the federal government announced, effective July 2008, that it would require all immigrants to obtain the Gardasil vaccination as a condition of immigration. Immigrant, health and women's advocacy groups protested the rule, and the Alliance Defending Freedom (formerly the Alliance Defense Fund) filed a lawsuit. In response, in November of that year, the CDC reversed course and announced that the HPV vaccine should not be required for immigration.

The Government's Reversal

Consistent with the state's obligation to protect life, in previous years, the *Parens Patriae* doctrine was used to require parents to consent to life-sustaining medical treatment, such as life-saving antibiotics or blood transfusions, for their child, despite objections based on religious or non-religious grounds. In 1984, Congress enacted a law to prohibit facilities receiving monies under the Child Abuse Protection and Treatment Act from denying care to a disabled infant simply because of that disability, regardless of the parents' desires.

With the growing strength of the euthanasia movement in the U.S. however, it should surprise no one that many doctors have abandoned parents who were attempting to keep their sick children alive. Sadly, many courts and state legislatures have abandoned them as well.

In 1994, Baby Ryan Nguyen was born six weeks premature in Spokane, Washington. The doctors, believing that the baby's life was not worth saving, refused to treat the child, despite pleas from Baby Ryan's mother. The mother sued. The court sided with the doctors, and Mrs. Nguyen found another hospital to treat Baby Ryan. He lived for several more years.

In 2004, in Houston, Texas, Wanda Hudson's son was born with a form of dwarfism that impaired his lung and chest cavity development. In November of that year, arguing that the care was futile, the doctors decided to shut off his ventilator. The mother sued. The courts, citing a futile care law in Texas, sided with the hospital. The hospital shut off the ventilator and the child died. Reportedly, this is the first case of its kind in the U.S. where a child's ventilator has been shut off over the objection of a parent.

A recent article in the *Journal of Medical Ethics* should cause further alarm. Arguing that parents inflict "suffering" and "torture" on their sick children, the authors conclude that doctors, not parents, should make health care decisions for ill children. Although penned by two pediatricians practicing in London, the disdain these authors have for parental authority in health care is eerily similar to the attitude of Baby Ryan's doctors. In that case, because Mrs. Nguyen refused to follow the doctors' advice and leave her child to die, the doctors at the hospital reported her to protective services for abuse and neglect.

Minors' Health Care Records

Parents' rights to access the health care records of their child, under many state laws, hinge on whether they have the right to consent to the services. In states, such as North Carolina, that allow minors to consent to sexually transmitted disease testing and treatment, pregnancy treatment, contraceptives, mental health treatment, alcohol treatment, and drug treatment, parents are not allowed access to those medical records unless the child gives consent.

Under the overarching federal privacy laws affecting medical records, commonly known as HIPPA, parents are not allowed access to records regarding treatments for which a minor can consent. Furthermore, according to the regulations, even if the parent has the right to consent to the minor's service, the parent may not have access to the records if the hospital or facility personnel "in the exercise of professional judgment" decides that it is not in the "best interest" of the child to release the information, the hospital or facility can refuse to do so."

Protecting Children

The research is indisputable. The family—a mother and father, married and committed to a lifelong relationship—is the best environment for the rearing of children. Former U.S. Secretary of Education William Bennett once called the family the "original Department of Health, Education and Welfare." It is within the family that children learn ethics, love, discipline, and good citizenship.

Happenstance does not dictate this result. Fit parents produce healthy, happy, productive children because parents have the authority to mold their children, unfettered by government interference. Crippling this authority will only hurt children.

Children's rights advocates retort that children have fundamental rights to make medical decisions themselves without parental consent or interference. Interestingly, most of the medical "treatments" for which parents are being denied the right to consent—alcohol and drug treatment, pregnancy and STD treatment, and abortion—are not "procedures," but the consequences of behavior that most parents would consider egregious. All of these situations, including mental health treatment, are ones that require the guiding hand of a parent who loves and protects their child. Excluding parents denies them the fundamental right to care for their own children, and undermines the familial bond, which, as one legal scholar has written, "is vital to a child's sense of becoming and being an adult in his own right."

An often-cited reason for minor consent is that parents will mistreat or abuse their children if they find out their child is engaging in sexual activity, pregnant, or using drugs. The statistics do not support this conclusion. In "Parental Involvement in Minors' Abortion Decision," most parents suffered emotional distress in finding out their child had an abortion. Only one percent of those children surveyed suffered physical violence at home. Less than 0.5 percent of the respondents were beaten. While these acts are shameful, they are the exception and not the norm, and the actions of parents in a few extreme cases should not be used to rob all parents of their God-given authority to raise their children as they see fit.

Crippling Parents and Freedom

A free society depends on a moral citizenry. That moral citizenry depends on the family, where a child learns love, forgiveness, charity, ethics, discipline, and as U.S. Supreme Court Justice Clarence Thomas stated in a 2011 dissenting opinion, "a capacity for self-government that would prepare a child for the outside world." The family is the heartbeat of freedom.

History has proven that strong families are the enemy of tyrannical governments. Communists, such as Karl Marx, believed that the family must be dismantled because it impedes economic equality and oppresses women.

Government can destroy the family in two ways: 1) By legally destroying the institution of marriage, which is the vessel from which healthy children grow; or 2) by destroying parental rights, leaving the family as nothing more than a hollow shell which can be crushed by the heel of the state.

No Retreat

T.S. Eliot once wrote:

> If we take the widest and wisest view of a Cause, there is no such thing as a Lost Cause, because there is no such thing as a Gained Cause. We fight for lost causes because we know that our defeat and dismay may be the preface to our successors' victory, though that victory itself will be temporary; we fight rather to keep something alive than in the expectation that it will triumph.

The cause to protect the rights of parents to make critical decisions in the raising and care of their own children seems insurmountable, but is not a battle that is won or lost overnight. The first step in restoring to parents the right to care for their own children must be taken now. North Carolinians should demand that the law be changed to return to parents the right to provide written, notarized consent before their child receives an abortion, contraceptives, or testing and treatment for STDs, mental health, drugs and alcohol.

For the sake of this nation's beloved children and posterity, retreat is not an option.

Organizations to Contact

The editors have compiled the following list of organizations concerned with the issues debated in this book. The descriptions are derived from materials provided by the organizations. All have publications or information available for interested readers. The list was compiled on the date of publication of the present volume; the information provided here may change. Be aware that many organizations take several weeks or longer to respond to inquiries, so allow as much time as possible.

Advocates for Youth

2000 M Street NW, Suite 750
Washington, DC 20036
(202) 419-3420 • fax: (202) 419-1448
website: www.advocatesforyouth.org

Advocates for Youth is an organization working in both the United States and developing countries that focuses on the sexual and reproductive health of teens. Programs it supports enable youth to make decisions about their sexual health in an informed and responsible way. The vision of Advocates for Youth reflects the group's core values: "Rights. Respect. Responsibility." Advocates for Youth publishes numerous informational essays available at its website, including "Emergency Contraception: A Safe and Effective Contraceptive Option for Teens."

American Center for Law and Justice (ACLJ)

P.O. Box 90555
Washington, DC 20090
(800) 296-4529
website: www.aclj.org

The American Center for Law and Justice (ACLJ) is dedicated to protecting religious freedom, which it views as a God-given right, in the United States and worldwide. It litigates, advocates, provides free legal services, and offers advice to individuals and governments concerning many issues. The group has represented clients before the US Supreme Court and in other federal courts. ACLJ has numerous memos and position papers available at its website and radio recordings, including "Birth Control and Minors."

American Civil Liberties Union (ACLU)
125 Broad Street, 18th Floor
New York, NY 10004
(212) 549-2500
e-mail: infoaclu@aclu.org
website: www.aclu.org

The American Civil Liberties Union (ACLU) is a national organization whose mission is to defend Americans' civil rights as guaranteed in the US Constitution and laws. The ACLU works in courts, legislatures, and communities to guarantee First Amendment rights, the right to equal protection, the right to due process, and the right to privacy. The ACLU publishes the semi-annual newsletter *Civil Liberties Alert* as well as briefing papers supporting abortion rights and access to birth control, among other reproductive health issues.

Center for Reproductive Rights
120 Wall Street
New York, NY 10005
(917) 637-3600 • fax: (917) 637-3666
e-mail: info@reprorights.org
website: www.reproductiverights.org

The Center for Reproductive Rights is a global legal advocacy organization dedicated to reproductive freedom, which it views as a basic human right that governments worldwide must protect and advance. The group litigates inside and outside the United States, engages policymakers regarding reproductive rights, and trains lawyers worldwide. The Center for Reproductive Rights publishes articles, reports, and briefing papers, among which is the article "The Contraception Controversy: A Comprehensive Reply."

Children's Healthcare Is a Legal Duty, Inc. (CHILD, Inc.)

136 Blue Heron Place
Lexington, KY 40511
(859) 255-2200
website: www.childrenshealthcare.org

Children's Healthcare Is a Legal Duty, Inc. (CHILD, Inc.) is a nonprofit organization dedicated to ensuring that children are protected from religion-based medical neglect and other religious and cultural practices that harm them. It advocates for laws requiring preventive care, diagnosis, and treatment of children regardless of the family's religious beliefs. CHILD, Inc. publishes a newsletter four times a year, which is available at its website.

Concerned Women for America (CWA)

1015 15th Street, NW, Suite 1100
Washington, DC 20005
(202) 488-7000
website: www.cwfa.org

Concerned Women for America (CWA) is a public policy women's organization focused on promoting Biblical values and combating secularism among citizens and in the public sphere through prayer, education, and action. The group's core issues include sanctity of life, defense of family, education, religious liberty, national sovereignty, sexual exploitation, and support for Israel. Among the brochures, fact sheets, and articles available on CWA's website is "Abortion Drugs Compliments of Neighbors and Friends."

Guttmacher Institute

125 Maiden Lane, 7th Floor
New York, NY 10038
(212) 248-1111 • fax: (212) 248-1951
website: www.guttmacher.org

The Guttmacher Institute conducts social science research, educates the public, and performs policy analysis with the goal of protecting and ensuring sexual and reproductive health and rights around the world. It researches sexual activity, contraception, abortion, and childbearing, publishes three journals, and offers extensive information on its website. The Institute's monthly publications *State Policies in Brief* provide information on legislative and judicial actions affecting reproductive health, such as the recent brief "An Overview of Minors' Consent Law."

National Center for Youth Law (NCYL)

405 14th Street, 15th Floor
Oakland, CA 94612
(510) 835-8098
website: www.youthlaw.org

The National Center for Youth Law (NCYL) legislates on behalf of low-income children. Focusing on child welfare economic security, health/mental health, and juvenile justice, NCYL aims to ensure that children receive adequate resources, support, and opportunities so that their future lives will be healthy and productive. NCYL publishes a quarterly legal journal, *Youth Law News*.

National Youth Rights Association (NYRA)

1101 15th Sttreet, NW, Suite 200
Washington, DC 20005
(202) 835-1739
website: www.youthrights.org

Led by youths, NYRA is a national nonprofit organization whose goal is to end age discrimination against young people and ensure their civil rights and liberties. NYRA's ten thousand members, from all fifty states, advocate for lower voting and drinking ages, repeal of curfew laws, and protection of student rights.

For Further Reading

Books

Sarah Elliston, *The Best Interests of the Child in Healthcare*. New York: Routledge-Cavendish, 2007.

Angel M. Foster and Lisa L. Wynn, eds., *Emergency Contraception: The Story of a Global Reproductive Health Technology*. New York: Palgrave Macmillan, 2012.

Melissa Haussman, *Reproductive Rights and the State: Getting the Birth Control, RU-486, Morning-After Pills and the Gardasil Vaccine to the US Market*. Santa Barbara, CA: Praeger, 2013.

David L. Hudson, *The Right to Privacy*. New York: Chelsea House, 2010.

Catriona Macleod, *'Adolescence,' Pregnancy, and Abortion: Constructing a Threat of Degeneration*. New York: Routledge, 2010.

Elaine Tyler May, *America and the Pill: A History of Promise, Peril, and Liberation*. New York: Basic Books, 2010.

Shawn Francis Peters, *When Prayer Fails: Faith Healing, Children, and the Law*. New York: Oxford University Press, 2007.

Heather Munro Prescott, *The Morning After: A History of Emergency Contraception in the United States*. New Brunswick, NJ: Rutgers University Press, 2011.

Jay Sicklick, *Adolescent Health Care: Legal Rights of Teens*. Hartford, CT: Center for Children's Advocacy, 2011.

Rickie Solinger, *Reproductive Politics: What Everyone Needs to Know*. New York: Oxford University Press, 2013.

Periodicals and Internet Sources

Priscilla Alderson, Katy Sutcliffe, and Katherine Curtis, "Children's Competence to Consent to Medical Treatment," *Hastings Center Report*, November–December 2006. www.thehastingscenter.org.

Jessica R. Arons, "Misconceived Laws: The Irrationality of Parental Involvement Requirements for Contraception," *William and Mary Law Review*, March 2000. http://wmlaw review.org.

Seth M. Asser and Rita Swan, "Child Fatalities From Religion-motivated Medical Neglect," *Pediatrics*, April 1, 1998. http://pediatrics.aappublications.org.

Heather Boonstra and Elizabeth Nash, "Minors and the Right to Consent to Health Care," *Guttmacher Report on Public Policy*, August 2000. http://www.guttmacher.org.

Caitlin Borgmann, "Abortion Parental Notice Laws: Irrational, Unnecessary, and Downright Dangerous," *Jurist*, July 27, 2009. www.jurist.org.

Erika Christakis, "The Argument You *Don't* Hear About Birth Control in Schools," *Time*, September 26, 2012. http://time.com.

Sherry F. Colb, "Can Religious Faith Justify Reckless Homicide? A Wisconsin Prosecution Raises Larger Issues," *FindLaw*, February 4, 2009. www.findlaw.com.

Melinda T. Derish and Kathleen Vanden Heuvel, "Mature Minors Should Have the Right to Refuse Life-Sustaining Medical Treatment," *Journal of Law, Medicine, and Ethics*, Summer 2000.

Caroline Fraser, "Suffering Children and the Christian Science Church," *Atlantic*, April 1995. www.theatlantic.com.

Rebecca Gudeman, "The *Ayotte* Opinion: Implications for New Hampshire and Other States," *Youth Law News*, January–March 2006. www.youthlaw.org/publications/yln.

Deena Guzder, "When Parents Call God Instead of the Doctor," *Time*, February 5, 2009. http://time.com.

Kristin Henning, "The Fourth Amendment Rights of Children at Home: When Parental Authority Goes Too Far," *William and Mary Law Review*, October 2011. http://wmlawreview.org.

Tara L. Kuther, "Medical Decision-Making and Minors: Issues of Consent and Assent," *Adolescence*, Summer 2003.

Rich Lowry, "Schools for Contraception," *National Review Online*, September 25, 2012. www.nationalreview.com.

Janna C. Merrick, "Spiritual Healing, Sick Kids, and the Law: Inequities in the American Healthcare System," *American Journal of Law and Medicine*, Summer–Fall 2003.

Jonathan Merritt, "Misguided Faith Healers Should Go to Jail," *Jonathan Merritt on Faith and Culture*, May 31, 2013. www .religionnews.com.

NARAL Pro-Choice America, "Mandatory Parental-Involvement Laws Threaten Young Women's Safety," January 1, 2013. www.naral.org.

Shawn Francis Peters, "Abusing Children in the Name of God," *OnFaith*, January 2, 2008. www.faithstreet.com/onfaith.

Sara Rosenbaum, Susan Abramson, and Patricia MacTaggart, "Health Information Law in the Context of Minors," *Pediatrics*, January 2009.

Lainie Friedman Ross, "Health Care Decisionmaking by Children—Is It in Their Best Interest?" *Hastings Center Report*, November–December 1997. www.thehastingscenter.org.

Joseph J. Sabia and Daniel I. Rees, "The Effect of Parental Involvement Laws on Youth Suicide," *Economic Inquiry*, January 2013.

Wesley J. Smith, "Abortion Now More Important than Parental Rights," *First Things*, March 24, 2010. www.firstthings.com.

Rita Swan, "Letting Children Die for the Faith," *Free Inquiry*, Winter 1998.

Rob Waters, "Medicating Amanda," *Mother Jones*, May/June 2005.

Robert Weitzel, "Sacrificing Children on the Altar of Parents' Fanatical Faith," *Freethought Today*, May 2008.

Index

A

Abortion
  antiabortion demonstrations,
    38, 112
  consent for, 4
  help in obtaining of, 45–47
  judicial bypass requirement,
    45–46
  minors' rights to, 12, 14–15
  pregnant minors and, 46–47
  TRAP laws, 46
  See also Parental consent for
    abortion; Parental involve-
    ment laws for abortion
Abrahamson, Shirley S., 69–81
Absence of certainty, 90–91
Addington v. Texas (1979), 57
Age of majority, 4, 17, 33, 64–65
Alcohol abuse, 4, 16, 64, 114
Alcohol treatment, 115, 119, 121
American Psychiatric Association,
  57
Americans United for Life (AUL),
  39, 41
Asser, Seth M., 102

B

Bartley v. Kremens (1977), 53
Bellotti v. Baird (1979), 4, 26–34, 39
Bennett, William, 119
Bergmann, Allyson, 86
Blackfeet Indian Reservation, 105
Blackstone, William, 111
Boonstra, Heather, 13
Brennan, William J., Jr., 19–25
Burger, Warren E., 48–58

C

California Department of Health
  Services, 91

Cardwell v. Bechtol (1987), 66
*Carey v. Population Services
  International* (1977), 4, 19–25
Cheng, Juliet, 89
CHILD (Children's Healthcare Is a
  Legal Duty, Inc.), 104
Child Abuse Protection and
  Treatment Act (1984), 118
Christian Science/Scientists, 5, 86,
  87, 101–104
Consent by Minors to Medical
  Operations Act (IL), 64, 67
Contraceptives, minors' access to
  constitutional rights, 22–23
  overview, 19–20
  parens patriae power and,
    115–117
  parental rights and, 113–114
  right to privacy, 19–25
  teen sex and, 23–25
  teens and, *21, 24*
Court-ordered treatment, 84–89,
  108, 113

D

Denton, E.G., 60–68
Denton, Rosie, 60
DepoProvera, 114
Divorced minors, 17
Doctor-patient relationship, 12
Drug abuse, 4
Due Process Clause (US
  Constitution), 20, 58

E

Eddy, Mary Baker, 101
Eisenstadt v. Baird (1972), 20, 23
Eliot, T.S., 121
Emancipated minors, 4, 12, 17, 68,
  113

Emancipation of Mature Minors
   Act (IL), 63, 65

F

Fair and equitable standard, 92–93
Faith Tabernacle Congregation
   (Philadelphia, PA), 104
Family planning by minors, 14–15
Fifth Amendment (US
   Constitution), 84
First Amendment (US
   Constitution), 28–29, 92, 108
First Century Gospel Church
   (Philadelphia, PA), 104
First Church of Christ, Scientist, 5
   See also Christian Science/
      Scientists
Florida Supreme Court, 86–87
Followers of Christ, 103
Fourteenth Amendment (US
   Constitution), 20, 27, 50, 84, 108

G

*Gale Encyclopedia of Everyday
   Law*, 11–18
Gardasil vaccine, 110, 115–117
Ginsberg v. New York (1968),
   28–29, 31
Goss v. Lopez (1975), 28
Great bodily harm, defined, 77
Guttmacher Institute, 114

H

Haas-Wilson, D., 37
Harned, Mary E., 35–44
Hauser, Colleen, 95, *98*
Hauser, Daniel, 95
Health care for minors
   debate over, 12
   dilemma over, 13
   emancipation impact, 4, 17
   exceptions to, 15–17
   expanded rights of, 11–18

family planning, 14–15
   informed consent doctrine,
      12–14
   introduction, 4–6
   overview, 12
   See also Mature minors and
      health care; Parental medical
      rights over minors; Religious
      exemption for medical
      treatment
Health care records, 119
Hermanson, Amy, 5, 6
Hermanson v. State (1992), 5
Hester, Tina, 45–47
HIPPA laws, 119
HIV testing, 16, 110, 114–115
Homicidal failure to provide care,
   79–81
HPV vaccine, 110, 115–117
   See also Gardasil vaccine
Huckabee, Mike, *32*
Hudson, Wanda, 118

I

Informed consent doctrine, 12–14
In Heinemann's Appeal (1880), 83
In re E.G. (1989), 59–68
In re Estate of Brooks (1965), 63
In re Estate of Longeway (1989),
   66, 67
In re Gault (1967), 22, 27, 28
In re Hamilton (1983), 67
In re Roger S. (1977), 58
In the Matter of B.S. (2003), 43–44
Involuntary hospitalization, state
   laws, 55*t*

J

Jehovah's Witnesses, 5, 60–68, *61*,
   83, 84, 85, *85*
*Jehovah's Witnesses in the State of
   Washington et. al. v. Kings County
   Hospital Unit No. 1* (1967), 83–84

Journal of Medical Ethics, 118
Judicial bypass requirement
    abortion help through, 45–46
parental involvement laws and,
    39–40, *41,* 43–44

K

Kent v. United States (1966), 28
Kupsch, Debra, 104–105

L

Laubenberg, Jodie, 46, 47
Luther, Martin, 99

M

Married minors, 17, 64–65
Marx, Karl, 120
Mathews v. Eldridge (1976), 50
Mature minor doctrine, 4, 17–18,
    115
Mature minors and health care
    ability to consent, 63–65, *64*
    constitutional and common law,
        65–66
    importance of maturity, 63–64
    judicial consideration, 66–68
    overview, 60
    refusal of treatment, 60–63
    right to consent and refuse,
        59–68
    See also Parental medical rights
        over minors
May v. Anderson (1953), 27
McAtee, Jane, 61
McCauley, Elisha, 84
McKeiver v. Pennsylvania (1971), 28
Medicaid, 47, 114
Medical emergency exception, 4,
    40–42
Medical records, confidentiality, 18
Mental health care of minors
    child's interests, 50–51
    conflict of interests, 53–54

Due Process Clause and, 48–58
    introduction, 4, 16
    involuntary hospitalization, 55*t*
    neutral factfinder needed with,
        57–58
    overview, 49
    parent's interests, 51–53
    right to admit, 111
    state procedures and, 49–50
    state role in, 56–57
Meyer v. Nebraska (1923), 54
Mohler, R. Albert, Jr., 94–99
Moore v. East Cleveland (1977), 27
Morning-after pills, 114
Myers, Charles and Merilee, 87

N

Nash, Elizabeth, 13
Neff, Ariel, 74
Neumann, Dale R., 70–81, *78*
Neumann, Leilani E., 70–81, *78,*
    95–96
Neumann, Madeline Kara, 70–81,
    95–96
Newington Children's Hospital
    (Poughkeepsie, NY), 89
Nguyen, Baby Ryan and mother,
    118

O

*Ohio v. Akron Center for
    Reproductive Health* (1990), 39

P

Parens patriae (parent of the na-
    tion) doctrine, 56, 67, 83, 89, 92,
    115–117
Parental consent for abortion
    avoidance of absolute veto,
        33–34
    cannot be absolute, 26–34
    constitutional rights of minors,
        27–28

Parental consent for abortion
(*continued*)
  limits on children's rights,
    28–30
  overview, 27
  parental involvement and,
    31–33
  role of parents, 30–31
  waiver, 15
Parental involvement laws for
  abortion
  benefits of, 36–37
  court decisions on, 37–39
  enhancements to, 41–42
  judicial bypass requirement,
    39–40, *41*, 43–44
  medical emergency exception,
    40–42
  overview, *29*, 35–36
  protection for minors and par-
    ents, 35–44
Parental medical rights over
  minors
  child protection and, 119–120
  diminishing of, 109–121
  foundation of, 110–111
  government control, 113–115,
    117–118
  health care records, 119
  mature minor doctrine and, 115
  overview, 110
  parens patriae doctrine and,
    115–117
  parental importance, 117
  protection of, 111–113
  rights of freedom, 120–121
Parental rights
  public opinion poll, *88*
  vs. religious rights, 73
Parham v. J.R. (1979), 48–58, *52*,
  111

Pediatrics (journal), 102–103
Perry, Rick, 45, 46, 47, 116
Physician bypass alternative, 15
Pierce v. Society of Sisters (1925),
  30, 51, 54
Planned Parenthood, *16*, 114
*Planned Parenthood of Central
  Missouri v. Danforth* (1976), 4,
  22–23, 31, 33–34, 54, 65
Planned Parenthood v. Casey
  (1992), 40
Powell, Lewis F., Jr., 26–34
*Prince v. Commonwealth of
  Massachusetts* (1944), 22, 30, 73,
  96, 97, 105, 108

R
Re Karwath (1972), 87
Religious exemption for medical
  treatment
  absence of certainty, 90–91
  biblical view of, 99
  care, providing of, 106–107
  child death and, 70, 95–96,
    102–103
  concern from family and
    friends, 72–74
  consequences of, 103–105
  court-ordered treatment, 84–89
  criminal prosecution, 86–87
  fair and equitable standard,
    92–93
  fair notice claim, 77
  homicidal failure to provide
    care, 79–81
  introduction, 5–6
  limits to, 97
  overview, 82–83, 101
  parents' argument in favor of,
    77–79
  parents cannot deny treatment,
    69–81, 94–99

personal narrative, 100–108
with preventative and diagnostic measures, 106
as protection for parental decisions, 82–93
rights of children, 107–108
right to, 105–107
spiritual healing belief, 70–71
state care and, 83–84, 89–90, 96–99
statutes for, 75–76
treatable conditions and, 74–75
treatment-through-prayer provision, 76–77
unfair treatment of parents, 91–92
worsening of illness, 71–72
Rights of children, 107–108
Roe v. Wade (1973), 20, 21, 23
Rogers, A.M., 82–93
Ross, Lainie Friedman, 117
Rutledge, Wiley Blount, 73
Ryan, Howard C., 59–68

S

Sexually transmitted diseases, 12, 16
Smith v. Organization of Foster Families (1977), 50
State v. Neumann (2013), 69–81
Stewart, Potter, 31
Summa, Mary, 109–121
Swan, Rita, 97, 100–108

T

Targeted regulation of abortion provider (TRAP) laws, 46
Teen sex, 23–25
Tennessee Supreme Court, 66
Thomas, Clarence, 120
Title X of the Health Care Services Act, 14–15, 114
Treatment-through-prayer provision, 76–77
Twitchell, David and Ginger, 86, 91
Twitchell, Robyn, 86

U

US Constitution. *See* Equal Protection Clause *and specific amendments*
US Government Office of Technology Assessment, 91
US Supreme Court, 18, 37, 84, 89, 108
See also specific court cases

W

Walker v. Superior Court (1988), 5
Whalen v. Roe, (1977), 20
Wisconsin v. Yoder (1972), 30
Wormgoor, Althea and Randall, 73–74

Y

Yachnin, Stanley, 60–61